Scattered Seeds

A Guide to
Jewish Genealogy

RJ Press
Boca Raton, Florida
✡✡✡

Notice of Liability

Every precaution has been taken in the preparation of this book. Neither the author nor any distributor will have any liability to any person or entity with respect to any loss or damage, caused or alleged to be caused directly or indirectly by the instructions contained in this book. Trademarks are used in an editorial fashion to the benefit of the trademark owner with no intention of infringement of the trademark.

Library of Congress: Cataloging in Publication Data 98-96477
Morris, Mona-Freedman
1. Genealogy
Scattered Seeds: A Guide to JewishGenealogy
i Includes Glossary
1-Jews-Genealogy-handbooks, manual, etc.

ISBN 0-9666590-0-7

Printed in the United States of America
First Printing

This book is dedicated to my parents, Hyman Freedman and Ruth Schwartz-Freedman. They have been my teachers and my inspiration.

To my daughters: Stacey, Barri and Gia and my son-in laws Adam and Michael.

To Rebecca and Josh: the newest branches on the family tree.

To Mori and Carol - without whose encouragement this book would never have been completed.

To the special friends I call family-

and to Donald - for everything.

"There are two lasting gifts
we can give to our children.
One is roots, the other wings"

Old Chinese Proverb

TABLE OF CONTENTS

Preface

List of Maps

List of Illustrations

Preface

This guide is designed to teach the novice researcher how to trace and record his or her family history. The reader is taken step by step through the often confusing process of amassing records. *Italics* are used to alert the reader that explanations to italicized phrases are available in the glossary.

Time saving tips appear throughout the book. Included in the research will be 'how to':

- □ Search for vital records
- □ Find and research census records
- □ Search Naturalization records
- □ Search Passenger Arrival records
- □ Prepare an oral history
- □ Search early nineteenth century records
- □ Find your ancestral towns
- □ Harness the Internet for research

You are the best and most knowledgeable person to research your family. You have hidden memories that will enable you to recognize a record even if the names are slightly wrong. Take the time and record your own personal history now.

Common Misconceptions

All Jewish records were destroyed or lost in the Holocaust

All the records were not destroyed during World War II. The Nazis kept records, as did captive Jews. Records were hidden in ingenious places. Examples are those found in the Ringelblum Milk Can buried beneath the ground of the Warsaw Ghetto. Many Holocaust records are available on microfilm and microfiche. They have recently become available on the Internet as well.

These records are available to **YOU**!

My family is not interested in the past

Just the opposite is usually true. As you uncover information about your ancestors,   you will find that almost *everyone* in your family is interested. I have never found enthusiasm lacking once information was shared amongst other family members. And, given the opportunity,   family members will share their knowledge of family facts eagerly.

The memories of the older family members are gone.

Many persons with memory disorders can recall events with clarity that happened 50 or more years ago.

There is plenty of time.

Time is the enemy of all genealogists. The information that can be passed along by an older relative might take you months or years to locate without their participation. A relative might know the Port of Entry used by your ancestors when they first arrived in this country. This person might know in which cemeteries family members are buried, have birth certificates and other information you seek. These same family members might know the whereabouts of other family members you may not be aware exist.

"Genealogy"

"The study of ancestry or family lineage."
Webster's Dictionary

A genealogist or family historian traces the various lines of the family's lineage and shows these findings by means of genealogical charts or trees.

Genealogy is your gift of heritage
from one generation to another.

Each genealogical search for information is different. You may want to document the names of all the direct descendants of one or more of your ancestors. Another option would be to write an in depth portrait of your entire family. You may want to chart a family tree containing three, eight or sixteen generations. Each person must define the parameters of his/her search. This search can and usually does change as you attain more knowledge.

There are more records available today than ever before. The disintegration of the Soviet Union has given access to an abundance of records previously denied to the genealogist.

The time is Now!

Introduction

Why did your ancestors leave the "old country"? For most Jews, it was both religious and economic persecution. Sholem Aleichem's fictional character Tevye from *Tevye the Milkman (Fiddler on the Roof)* is typical of constant conflicts that were occurring throughout Europe.

Jewish migration differed from other nationalities. When the *emigrant*[1] left, he knew that there would be little chance of his returning "home." This would be the last time he saw family members. The following is typical of an emigrant's plight.

Rashka Wilenshelsky and Isaac Schwartz left their native countries of Romania and Russian occupied Poland for two separate and distinct reasons.

Isaac was born September 18, 1869 in *Iasi (Jassy)* Romania before hereditary surnames were common. He was an educated, merchant class Romanian Jew. Isaac read and spoke five languages. His family had vineyards and wineries in *Moldavia*. They also participated in the profitable Oriental carpet trade.

Isaac lived in a country where the right to work was taken away as government policy. The government was then able to declare these same persons indigent and oust them from the country. To draw attention to their dire circumstances, many of these Romanian Jews walked across Europe publicizing their plight. These Jews were known as Feygusers.

Rashka grew up in Bialystok, Poland. Jewish settlements had existed there prior to 1558. During the Second Polish Census (1932) Bialystok listed its city population as 92,000 people of which 39,000 were Jews. As of 1994, the Jewish population of Bialystok was one.

---

[1] *Emigrant*-one who leaves home to resettle in another country

Rashka's family was also of the merchant class. Her mother Leah died when Rashka was four years old. Her father Zalmon remarried and produced three more children with his second wife. Rashka and her stepmother did not get along. Rashka was twenty one years old when her boyfriend was drafted into the Czar's army. Typically, a draftee served thirty five years before being released and most Jews did not survive this conscription.

Events were happening fast. Rashka's cousin Matel Balberg had died during childbirth in America. Raska's father encouraged her to go to America and meet Matel's widower, Isaac Schwartz.

Isaac and Rashka were married August 26, 1900. Isaac died in 1950, Rashka in 1962.

Rashka was my grandmother and Isaac my grandfather. No one in my family was aware of any of the above information, including Raska's real name was Rachel, until I uncovered these facts through my research.

Your own family history is unique and special. Learn about it and from it. Preserve this legacy for your children, grandchildren and for all the generations that follow.

I gathered and documented this information by implementing the same research techniques contained in this guide.

If I can do it, so can you!

Clues To

Your Ancestry

"To understand today,

we must learn about

the past! "

History of Ancient Israel

*T*he ancestors of the Jews were originally known *as* the *Ivrim* or *Hebrews* (people from across the Euphrates River). The Patriarchs were Abraham, his son Isaac, and grandson Jacob, also known as Israel. The Matriarchs were Sarah (Abraham's wife), Rebecca (Isaac's wife), Leah and Rachel (Jacob's wives). Jacob had thirteen children, a daughter Dinah and twelve sons. The sons formed the original twelve tribes, *B'nai Israel* (Children of Israel), who left Egypt and journeyed to Palestine. The twelve tribes settled upon their own lands. Joseph's lands were divided between his two sons, Manasseh and Ephraim.

Reuben	Simeon	Levi
Judah	Dan	Naphtali
Gad	Asher	Issachar
Zebulun	Joseph	Benjamin.

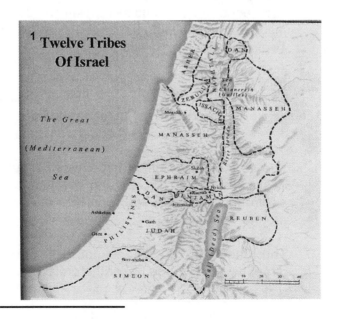

[1] Twelve Tribes Of Israel

---

[1] Holy Scriptures; Menorah Press; Chicago 1973

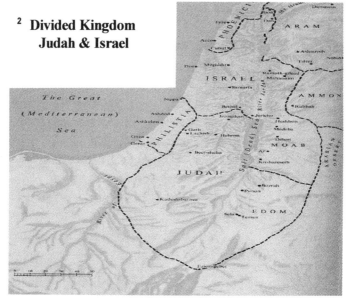

² **Divided Kingdom**
Judah & Israel

Kingdom of Israel

About 11ᵗʰ century, B.C.E.(Before the Common Era) the twelve tribes united under one King, Saul, who was succeeded by David and then Solomon. Jerusalem was made the capital of the united Israel and the First Temple was built.

After the death of Solomon the northern ten tribes united forming the Kingdom of Israel, with it's capital Samaria. While the two southern tribes formed the Kingdom of Judah (House of David), keeping it's capital Jerusalem.

The northern kingdom of Israel was conquered by the Assyrian's in 722 B.C.E. and most of the Israelites assimilated within the local population of Assyria. These are the *Ten Lost Tribes*.

The Kingdom of Judah was not destroyed like that of Israel because it was under the protection of Egypt. In

---

² Ibid.

587 B.C.E. the Babylonians conquered Judah and destroyed the Temple. Ten thousand Jews from Jerusalem were taken as prisoners to Babylonia. This period is known as the Babylonia Exile. The Jews continued to practice their religion and 586 B.C.E. King Cyrus of the Persian Empire defeated the Babylonians. He allowed the exiled Jews to return home (*aliyah*) and rebuild the Temple. Many Jews decided to stay in Babylonia and this was the first Diaspora (Scattering). The returning Jews built the Second Temple in 515 B.C.E. and held the first *Rosh Hashanah* in 445 B.C.E.

Alexander the Great defeated the Persians and Palestine came under the rule of Syria. Religious persecution under King Anticus caused a rebellion led by Judah the Maccabee (Hammer). In 142 B.C.E. Palestine again became an independent Jewish state.

The Romans invaded and conquered Palestine and in 70 C.E. destroyed the Second Temple. Many of the Jews were sold into slavery by 73 C.E.

The Diaspora

The Babylonian Exile was the First Diaspora and Jews were living in every civilized country outside Palestine by 70 C.E. (Common Era). Life for the Jew changed when the Roman Empire accepted Christianity (4th century C.E.) and major persecutions of Jews were commonplace.

Over the next five hundred years Jews were expelled from different towns, cities, and countries. In Italy, a wall was erected to separate Jews from the general population (ghetto). Laws were passed regulating the way of life of Jews; land could no longer be owned and working in many of the trades or crafts was practically eliminated. Jews were labeled as "inferior". Many countries required Jews to wear distinguishing clothing. Migrations from Spain and Central Europe began as the persecutions increased.

New centers of learning were established in Poland, Russia and Lithuania by those fleeing the oppression in central Europe and Spain. As in previous centuries, the lands that offered freedom and welcomed them eventually had persecutions and expulsions of their own.

The next center for the fleeing Jews was Neuw Amsterdam (New York) in America. The first migration had been the Spanish Jews during the Inquisition in 1492. The next large migration began at the beginning of the nineteenth century. By 1880 there were more than 250,000 German Jews in the United States. They resided predominately in New York, Philadelphia, Pittsburgh, Chicago, Baltimore and Cleveland.

By 1880, what was to become the greatest emigration ever began. Jews came from Eastern Europe, from the lands known as Russian-Poland, the Austro-Hungarian Empire and Romania. Due to restrictive laws enacted in the United States, Jewish immigration to America had slowed to a trickle by the 1920's. The final large waves of immigrants came prior to and just after WWII.

---

[3] U. of So. Florida "A Teacher's Guide to the Holocaust"; 1997

Geographic Clues

Assume you have no idea of the geographic origins of your ancestors. You will now be shown how to find the general geographic area your ancestors came from.

Sephardi, Ashkanazi

The Ashkanazim and the Sephardim makeup the two predominant groups of Jews today. Are you Sephardi or Ashkanazi?

Sephardim

Sephardim, which means Spaniards in Hebrew, trace their ancestry to Spain, Portugal, and North Africa. Driven out during the Inquisition in 1492, the Sephardim sought refuge in the lands of North Africa, parts of the Turkish Empire, the Balkans, the Caribbean and the Americas. Many fled to European towns that already contained large Ashkenasi populations. The Sephardim and Ashkenasim retained their own customs and traditions. Ladino, the Sephardic language, is Spanish with Hebraic letters.

---

[4] J.B. Bury "Atlas to Freeman's Historical Geography" Longmans Green & Co; 1903 3rd Edition

Ashkanazim

Ashkenazim is the Hebrew word for Germans, Yiddish, their language, is a dialect of German written with Hebraic letters. The majority of Jews today in America and Europe are of Ashkenazi descent. The Ashkenazi originated in tenth century Germany and Northern France.

Customs Cans Be Clues

☐	The blowing of a shofar during a funeral = Sephardic
☐	The placing of earth from the Holy Land at a burial = Ashkanazi
☐	A two-day Rosh Hashana = Ashkanazi
☐	Kissing of the prayer book during services = Ashkanazi
☐	Marriage brokers (shadchan) = Ashkanazi
☐	Rice served at Passover = Sephardic
☐	Naming a child for a living relative = Sephardic

[5]Barnaui, Eli Historical Atlas of the Jewish People; C. Hachette Litterature

Jewish Naming Practices

Sephardim

The Sephardim name the eldest son after the paternal grandfather. The eldest daughter is named after the paternal grandmother. The second male child is named after the maternal grandfather, while the second female child is named for the maternal grandmother. The next male children are named alternatively for the paternal uncles and aunts, and maternal uncles and aunts.

Ashkenazi

The practice of naming children in honor of a deceased relative is believed to have begun with the ancient Egyptians. The royal family and their descendants were the only persons permitted to name a child after the dead.

Test this theory.

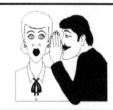 Tell your relative "I would like to name my soon-to-be-born child after you." If they turn pale, and clutch their heart, you are probably an Ashkenazi. To an Ashkenazi, naming a child after a living person is the same as saying "I wish you dead."

The use of Hebrew names disappeared over the centuries, until in the twelfth century, rabbis mandated that a Hebrew name must be given at the time of circumcision. This mandate led to the resurgence of biblical names. The use of two given names became a the custom. A Hebrew name was used for religious events and a secular name for civil events. This practice continues today. i.e. Zvi Hersh, Manasseh Manis, Stacey Sarah.

Hapsburg Emperor Karl VI of the Austro-Hungarian Empire passed the Familiants Law in 1726. This law was intended to decrease the number of Jews by only allowing the oldest son to marry. Many of the younger sons moved to different villages and/or assumed the bride's surname in order to marry.

Then in 1797, the Hapsburg Emperor Joseph II allowed Jews to adopt biblical surnames. Jews modified these names to the German language. Judah meaning lion was translated into Low/Loeb. Naphtali meaning deer was translated into Hart in German, Hirsch in Yiddish and Cerf in French.

Special names were often given to children born on or around holidays. The name Esther or Malka (queen) can indicates a birth during Purim.

Czar Alexander I of Russia attempted to get Polish Jews to adopt surnames in 1804. The Jews resisted, fearing that identification would lead to taxation and military conscription. Polish Jews did not assume hereditary surnames until after 1836. It has been reported that in the countries within the Turkish empire, hereditary surnames were not in effect until well after 1870.

The Czarist conscription laws permitted only the oldest son to be exempt from military service. Many younger sons were "adopted" by families without sons and assumed the new family's name to avoid military service.

Beautiful names such as Gold or Silver usually required bribery. If the official did not like the individual, they might be given the negative name of Schnorer (pig).

Meaning of Names

Jewish names can indicate many things when analyzed. If a surname ends in er, you can trace the origin of the name to a location in Germany. i.e. Gredinger is from Greding, Germany. Slavic for "son of" is *wich* or *wicz*.

If your name ends in *kin or ov*, your origin may be Ukrainian. Most of the given names assumed by Jews fall into the following categories:

Biblical:
> Abraham, Isaac, Sarah, Rebecca

Post-Biblical:
> Included nickname or occupation
> i.e. Chaim the Schneider (the tailor)

Patronymic:
> Chaim *ben* Menashe

ben	=	son of (Hebrew)
ibn	=	son of (Arabic)
bar	=	son of (Aramaic)
bat	=	daughter of (Aramaic, Hebrew)

Acronyms:
> RASHI   = _Ra_bbi _SH_lomo ben _I_saac.

Geographic:

er	=	German - from the town of
sky	=	Slavic - from the town of
witz/ovitch	=	Slavic son of
kin	=	Ukrainian son of
de Leon	=	from Leon

Descriptive

Kluger	=	wise
Becker	=	baker
Geller	=	yellow (blond haired)
Schweid	=	a person from Sweden

While the language of trading amongst the Christian merchants was Latin, the language of trading amongst the Jews in Europe was Yiddish. A third language was needed to trade between Moslems, Jews, and Christians. This language was Turkic. [7]

Ever wonder why the surnames of Schwartz and Weiss are so prevalent? And, why Belarus was called White

_____

[7]Thumim, Donald; NY Times, 1990 Travel section

Russia? If we translate the German/Yiddish names into Turkic, we have:

Black, (Swarz) - North
White (Weiss) - West
Red (Roth) - South
Blue (Blau) - East

Therefore, White Russia is west of Mother Russia. A person from the North might be called Swarz (Schwartz).

Expulsion

The Jews were expelled from Germany, Spain and other Central European countries at the same time the lands to the east of Germany were being settled . A merchant middle class (burgher) was desperately needed to administer these lands. Poland-Lithuania and Austro-Hungary enticed the burgher class by offering free land, freedom of worship and economic opportunity to all. A large voluntary migration of the burgher class of Germany headed East.

While many Jews trace their ancestry directly to Germany, England, Iraq or Syria the majority of Jews today are the descendants of a specific area in Eastern Europe known as the *Pale of Settlement.*

The Pale of Settlement

The Pale of Settlement was a geographic restriction created in 1791 by Czarist Russia. This limitation designated where Jews were allowed to live, specifically which towns, villages and cities. The Pale was expanded as Russia conquered the lands known today as Belarus, (formerly White Russia), the Ukraine, Moldova (Bessarabia), Poland, Lithuania and parts of the Austro-Hungarian Empire.

Permission was required to live anywhere but in your family's assigned town, lease lands, keep taverns and attend secondary schools. Jews without special permits were subject to immediate arrest and/or death.. Eventually these limited rights were denied.

Taxes were doubled and imposed on essential items such as candles. Expulsions from the farmlands increased the population within cities.

Ninety-four (94%) of the people living within the Pale were Jews. The assassination of Czar Alexander II in 1881, with the *pogroms* (riots) that followed led to a massive emigration of nearly one third of the Eastern European Jews. In 1917 after the Communist Revolution, the Pale was abolished.

[8] Gilbert, Martin, - Jewish History Atlas; Collier Books 1969

Galicia

You can further define the Eastern European territory where your ancestors lived by determining if you are a *Litvak* or *a Galicianer*. Galicianers trace their ancestry to the territories of the former Austro-Hungarian Empire, southwestern Romania and southwestern Poland. Galicia is a historic region of Eastern Europe, located north of the Carpathian Mountains. It extends from Krakow (Poland) east to Ternopol (Ukraine). Annexed by Austria in the First Partition of Poland (1772), Galicia existed until 1918, as a separate province of the Austro-Hungarian monarchy. The dialect of *Yiddish* spoken was different in Galicia than in Lithuania. The Litvaks and Galicianers followed different rabbinical teachings and developed many different customs.

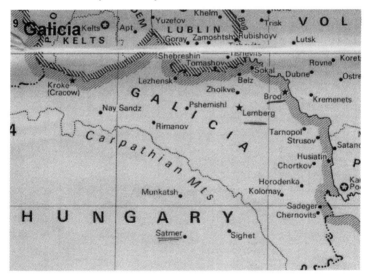

Duchy of Lithuania

Jews residing in the lands that constituted the Duchy of Lithuania were known as Litvaks. These countries

[9] The Shtetl Book; Roskies; KTAV Publishing 1975

today are: Lithuania, Belarus, Latvia, Estonia, Moldavia, Moldova (northeastern Romania), parts of Northern Poland and the Ukraine. The Duchy of Lithuania, was bounded by the Baltic Sea, Latvia, Belarus, Poland and the Russian enclave of Kaliningrad (Konigsberg). Rule was extended to include Belarus and the Ukraine between 1236-1386. This empire extended east as far as the Dnieper River and south to the Black Sea.

In 1386, Grand Duke Jagello married Jadwiga, Queen of Poland merging the two countries. In the 16th century Poland-Lithuania, formed the Union of Lublin (1569), creating a new federation. The new commonwealth, Lithuania became a province of Poland. In the 18th century the Polish kingdom was divided amongst Russia, Prussia, and Austria. As a result of the last partition of Poland (1795) and the post-Napoleonic settlement at the Congress of Vienna (1815), most of Lithuania was absorbed by Russia; the area along the Baltic coast was given to Prussia.

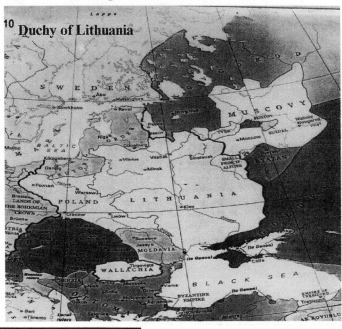

[10] The Times Atlas of European History; Harper & Collins

A competition and prejudice occurred between the Litvaks and the Galicianers. Each claimed that their group was superior to the other. Mothers were known to warn their daughters and sons not to intermarry.

"No good could come of a marriage between a Galicianer and a Litvak."

The foods consumed by each group differed as well. Litvaks tended toward more peppery foods, while Galicianer's used more sugar.

Does your family like sweet or tart gefilte fish?
Sweet is Galicia.   Tart is Litvak.

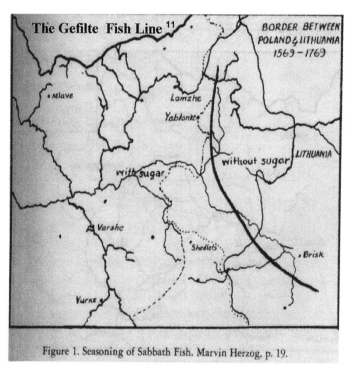

Figure 1. Seasoning of Sabbath Fish. Marvin Herzog, p. 19.

---

[11] Marvin Herzog The Yiddish Language in Northern Poland

The Key to

Unlocking

the Puzzle

FAMILY CHART

FOR ① _____

Your Name: _____
Your Hebrew Name: ② _____
            Paternal □
Named for Maternal □ ③ _____
Birth Date: ④_____ City: _____ County: _____ State: _____
 Marriage Date: ⑤_____ City: _____ County: _____ State: _____

⑥ FATHER'S NAME: _____
Hebrew Name: _____
Paternal □
Named for Maternal □ _____
Birth Date: _____ City: _____ County: _____ State: _____
Date of Death: _____ City: _____ County: _____ State: _____
Place of Burial: _____ City: _____ County: _____ State: _____
Date of Marriage: _____ City: _____ County: _____ State: _____
Other Marriages: _____

MOTHER'S NAME (at Birth): _____
Hebrew Name: _____
         Paternal □
Named for Maternal □ _____
Birth Date: _____ City: _____ County: _____ State: _____
Date of Death: _____ City: _____ County: _____ State: _____
Place of Burial: _____ City: _____ County: _____ State: _____
Other Marriages: _____

YOUR SPOUSE (Name at Birth): _____
Hebrew Name: _____
         Paternal □
Named for Maternal □ _____
Birth Date: _____ City: _____ County: _____ State: _____
Date of Death: _____ City: _____ County: _____ State: _____
Place of Burial: _____ City: _____ County: _____ State: _____
Other Marriages: _____

⑧ CHILDREN of _____(mother) & _____(father)

	NAME	BORN	TOWN	STATE/COUNTY	SPOUSE
1					
2					

Current Address:
  ① _____
      _____
  ② _____
      _____

What Is Data?

*D*ata is any and all the information you can collect. This information can be in the form of names, addresses, and telephone numbers. Data can be photographs, tombstone pictures, audio or video recordings. You will be shown how to collect federal, state and local governmental records.

Interview your oldest relatives first. Organizing your records can wait. Take random notes, make audio or video recordings, and put the material in a folder or loose-leaf binder until you are ready to review it.

Build on what you already know or suspect. Check family photo albums, noting the addresses of buildings, the dates and names of people in the pictures. Use a photographic pen to write on back of the pictures. These special pens can be purchased at photographic stores. Using a plain pen can cause loss of picture images. Make laser copies of any important photos, storing originals in acid free plastic sheets. The use plain plastic page sheets will protect notes enabling the handling of documents easily.

*Don't forget to check your **Safe Deposit Box** for documents.*

First determine what you already know about your family. The first form is the *Family Chart* that appeared on the preceding page. Fill out this form now.

① Write your name as it appeared at birth. i.e., *maiden name.*

② In this space write your Hebrew Name.

③ Write the name of the person for whom **you** were named. Be specific. *Paternal* means father.

named. Be specific. *Paternal* means father. *Maternal* means mother. i.e. If you were named for your mother's father you would write *maternal grandfather*.

④ Write the **date** of your birth, city, county and state. If you are unsure of the location, place a ? after your answer.

⑤. Fill in the requested information for your Father and Mother. List your mother's BIRTH name if known. If you are uncertain as to the dates use the abbreviations *abt.*(about) or *ca.* (circa) If you do not know the exact date of death, but know it was "around" Passover, Chanukah, etc. put that in with the appropriate abbreviated symbol

⑥ List the details about your spouse, if applicable.

Locating Data

A questionnaire is the easiest way to determine information. Adapt the following form to your requirements. Use this questionnaire for telephone or mail interviews. It will help you to be organized and professional when you approach relatives. Each question answered can lead to the discovery of previously unknown , but important documents and information.

Review the form carefully. Knowledge of a relative's Hebrew name and the person for whom they were named, will enable those of Ashkenazi descent to approximate the latest possible date of death for that ancestor. Check the given names of all cousins and follow the pattern of naming.

Initial interviews should be with your oldest and closest relatives. This will give you confidence when you approach newly discovered relatives.

Sample Family Questionnaire

You

    Your Birth NAME   _____

    Your Hebrew NAME _____

    For Whom were you named _____

    Your Birth Date   ____ _____ _____

    Birth Address _____

    Borough/City _____ County _____

Spouse

    Birth name of SPOUSE _____

       (in marriage that produced children)

    Hebrew NAME _____

    For Whom were you named _____

    Date of Birth _____

    Date of Marriage: _____ City _____ County _____

Other Marriages:

    Birth Name of SPOUSE _____

    Date of Marriage _____ City _____ County _____

> Requesting information about the person's spouse will enable you to obtain the date of marriage and other information about that person. Burial location questions may yield the names of other relatives buried in the same cemetery. Names and dates of previous marriages often will yield more information. Always request the person's name at birth. i.e. Ida often was Idel or even Adel before becoming Americanized.

Names of *Landsmanshaften* or Fraternal Organizations:

Name of Synagogue:

> You will be requesting the same information about your relative's father, mother, and grandparents. Ask the names of any religious affiliations, fraternal, or professional organizations they may have belonged to. *Landsmanshaften* were associations of persons from the same towns. They were created to benefit recent

immigrants by providing medical, social, immigration, and financial help. Burial arrangements were administered by these societies. Did your ancestors belong to any?

Paternal:

1895 Address   _____

1900 Address   _____

1905 Address   _____

1900 Address   _____

1910 Address   _____

1915 Address   _____

1920 Address   _____

1925 Address   _____

1930 Address   _____

Addresses can be of significant importance when searching for records. Due to the popularity of certain surnames, it may be difficult to find the exact person you are searching for. In your interview it was determined that "in 1920, we lived on the Lower East Side of New York, I think Stanton Street." This information can reduce the number of Harry Cohen's you will have to search. Divide your information by your Paternal (Father) and Maternal (Mother). The dates above are for the years Federal and State censuses were taken. See Federal Records Research for more information.

You want to contact the children of the relatives you have discovered. Knowing their names and addresses will save you time. These are your cousins and another generation. A full questionnaire appears in the Appendix.

It is now time to evaluate the information you have obtained. Fill in the Pedigree Chart on the next page. A *pedigree chart* lists the direct ancestors of one person in a graph format.

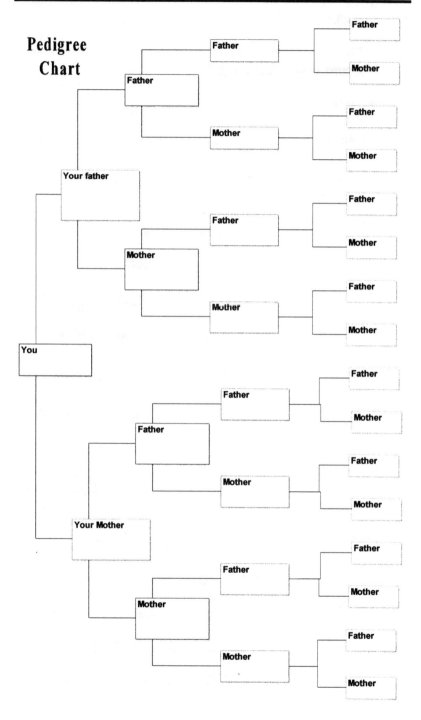

Pedigree Chart

Ahnetafel Chart

Fill in the *Ahnetafel Chart* below. Ahnetafel charts record your direct ancestors in text format.

Generation 1 : _____
You

Generation 2 : _____
①Your Father

_____
② Your Mother

Generation 3 : _____
③ Paternal Grandfather   (Father of ①)

_____
④ Paternal Grandmother   (Mother of ①)

_____
⑤ Maternal Grandfather   (Father of ①)

_____
⑥ Maternal Grandmother   (Mother of ①)

Generation 4: _____
⑦ Paternal Grandfather   (Grandfather of ①)

_____
⑧ Paternal Grandmother (Grandmother of ①)

_____
⑨ Maternal Grandfather   (Grandfather of ①)

_____
⑩ Maternal Grandmother (Grandfather of ①)

Generation 5: _____
⑩ Paternal Great-Grandmother (Mother of ④)

_____
①① Maternal Great-. Grandfather (Father of ⑤)

_____
①② Maternal great-grandmother (Mother of ③)

_____
①③ Maternal great-grandfather (Father of ⑥)

_____
①④ Maternal great-grandmother (Mother of ⑥)

Analyze the material you have collected. The material can consist of a family tree found in a bible or baby book or stories related by family members. You might have found documents in your attic, basement or safe deposit box.

How to locate your missing relatives

You want to find your mother's sister Yetta. Yetta lived in Brooklyn, NY in 1956. She would be 70 years old now. Assume your Aunt Yetta is still alive

① Your local library contains a selection of telephone directories (white pages). Look at the telephone directories where your aunt lived. If she still lives in the area and her telephone is listed, your search has come to a successful conclusion. Note the information (name, address, and telephone number). You can get the zip codes at your local post office.

② Aunt Yetta is not listed in the New York telephone directories. We reason she might have moved to the suburbs. Check the telephone directories for areas adjoining her last known residence. We do not find Aunt Yetta listed.

③ This is the computer age. Your local public library has a computer that will enable you to search for your missing relative easily. Take advantage of it and search its telephone directory *database*.

The United States telephone database contains over 80 million names, addresses and phone numbers. You can purchase telephone databases at your locale computer or office supply store.

If you subscribe to an *on-line service*, (Prodigy®, America-on-line®, etc.), you can search their databases of addresses right from your home. See Organizing Data and Computers.

④ Using the library's or your home databases, access the telephone directory. Yetta's surname is Cackin. Type the name Cackin. Check all persons with this surname. Yetta Cackin, her address, zip code, area code and telephone number appear within seconds.

The information in the databases is based on the published telephone directories. You can assume that the above information is less than one year old. This is fine for an unusual surname. What if Aunt Yetta's last name is Schwartz? We search and find hundreds of Schwartz's. How do you narrow your search?

Narrowing a telephone search

① Limit searches to the city she last resided in.

② Limit the search further to the first name of Uncle Sam, Aunt Yetta's husband.

③ Enlarge a search to include entire state, but limit area codes.

④ Use alternate spelling of the name. Aunt Yetta is now known as Ida. With names as popular as Cohen, Schwartz, Friedman, etc. you may have to send out additional search letters. Fortunately, most of us will have found our relative at this point.

⑤ Enter complete information onto the Address Directory and/or Correspondence Log in the Appendix.

Address directory and/or correspondence log

NAME	ADDRESS	CITIES, STATE, ZIP	TELEPHONE #	

Don't forget to check the Sunbelt states for older relatives. Many persons retire to warm weather: Florida, California and Arizona are good starts.

Correspondence Tips

Getting a person to respond to your letter is important. If you follow the guidelines below you are sure to get a positive reply.

> ❏ Write friendly but short, concise letters. Provide enough information to get a response.
> ❏ Request research of **indexed** records only. Non- indexed research requires hours of searching.
> ❏ Include a self-addressed, stamped envelope (SASE).
> ❏ Give a valid reason why you are requesting the information.
> ❏ Include donation or fee for requested service.

There are two main categories of letters. The first will be to a government agency or archive. Hire a professional researcher for unindexed files.

The second category is to relatives who may or may not even know of your existence. Limit your initial requests and provide them with the information on how you believe they are related to you.   Inclusion of a descendant's chart with your name and theirs highlighted will enable the recipient to see the possible connection. Announce in your letter that the recipient will be reimbursed for ALL costs related to your requests. Include any genealogical associations you belong to.

Sample Letter to Reference Library or Archive:

You will be writing to many archives and libraries for help. Use the letter below as a model for your own letter. Include in the letterhead your full name, address and telephone number, fax number and e-mail address if applicable.

Reference Librarian
XYZ Special Library
Washington, D.C. 90009

RE: 1914 City Directory for Harris Cackin

Dear Librarian:

> *I am involved in the research of the Morris Cackin family. They lived at 123 Town Road, Wichita, Kansas in 1914. Please inform me if your library has a local history or newspaper obituary indexes that might list this family. Any other information that you feel might be helpful in my quest to document this family would be appreciated.*
>
> *Enclosed is a self-addressed stamped envelope (SASE) for your convenience. In anticipation of your needing to photocopy indexes and/or documents, I have also included $3.00 to cover the initial expenses. If the cost exceeds this amount, please notify me.*
>
> *I would further appreciate if you could suggest other libraries or archives that might be helpful in my search. If any of this material is available through an inter- library loan, please inform me of this as well.*

Letter to a previously unknown relative:

> *Dear **Cousin** ,*
>
> *I am the daughter of Hyman Freedman and have been researching our family's ancestry. Recently I discovered through my research that you and I are both the descendants of **Aaron Lab Friedman**. To demonstrate this connection, I have included a self-explanatory chart. I have also enclosed a **questionnaire** with a **self addressed stamped envelope**. Please fill the information requested to the best of*

your knowledge. Your participation will enable me to continue my research. All dates of birth and marriage of living persons will be held in confidence upon your request.

*Of particular importance are any copies of immigration documents, (passports, naturalization certificates, etc.) from your **grandfather Morris** that might be in your possession. Additionally, copies of any correspondence between your family and the relatives in **Pruzhana, Belarus**, our ancestral town, would be of great interest. Names of persons and their addresses from that town are important, no matter how old they are.*

I am a member of (list genealogically related organizations you belong to)_____.

*As you can imagine, compiling all this information is a complicated task. I have amassed an enormous amount of data that I will share with you. Your participation is very important. **Enclosed is a family tree** for you and your family to keep. **A revised tree** will be mailed to you after I receive your completed questionnaire.*

*I will **reimburse you for all costs** related to reproduction of the above pictures and documents. Please notify me if these costs exceed $10.00.*

In the previous letter, the salutation COUSIN is used to establish the family connection. An offer of proof of connection is also included in the form of a family tree. The promise of a revised tree is the incentive for a prompt reply. **Definitely, do not ask for money.**

Always offer to reimburse the individual for copying expenses. You should include the mandatory *Self Addressed Stamped Envelope* (SASE) as a courtesy and to insure a reply.

Mailing your letter:

> On the line below your return address, include the words **Forwarding and Address Correction Requested.** The U.S. Postal Service will send you the address to which your letter has been forwarded for a total cost of 35¢, clearly a bargain price.

Interviewing relatives:

> You will be interviewing relatives to obtain more information. Listed below are sample questions. Tailor these questions to your requirements. When conducting an interview, consider video-taping. Remember to let the interviewee do the talking. Keep quiet while they collect their thoughts. Often, after a few minutes of thinking, your relative will come up with just the information you need. Limit your interview time. Remember that they are taking time out of their schedule to accommodate you.

Sample Questions

> Where were you born?
>
> Were you named after a family member? Who?
>
> Do you know the family's original surname? Was the name changed? When? Where?
>
> Are there other family members with your given name?
>
> Are there any family trees or books written about the family? Who gathered the information?
>
> Do you know their address?
>
> Are there any old pictures of the family? Who are the people? May I copy them?
>
> Where and when were the pictures taken?
>
> What languages did your parents speak?
>
> What newspapers did your parents read?
>
> What do you remember about the way the holidays were celebrated? (Rosh Hashanah, Chanukah, Purim, Yom Kippur, Passover)

Who were the first members of your family in the U.S.?
Where did they born? Exact pronunciation of towns
in Europe?

Did your relatives arrive in Canada first and then come
to the U.S.?

Why did they leave?   Pogroms, famine, draft?

Where did they live when they arrived?   And with
whom?

Did they have a large family?

Are there any family medical illnesses?

How old were they when they died?

Did they bring any unusual family heirlooms?
candlesticks, books, mortar and pestle

Do you resemble your mother, father or other family
member?

What occupations did your parents/grandparents have?

Do you remember being introduced to distant relatives,
perhaps at a funeral or Shiva? Who?

Describe the house where you were raised.
What chores did you do?   What was Shabbat dinner
like at your home?   What foods were served?

Was there a special food your mother made?

Did other relatives live nearby?

Were any of your relatives in any military service?
Which branch? Foreign or U.S.?

Are there any family organizations: Cousins clubs?

Is there a family cemetery or burial plot?   Are non
family members buried there?

Were any non-family members called cousin or aunt out
of respect?

Lawyers in the Family?

Check your local library for a copy of the seventeen volume
"Martindale-Hubbel Law Directory" This directory lists many
attorneys currently practicing Law.

Doctors in the Family?

The "American Medical Association Deceased Physician Master File" is a comprehensive list covering the years' 1906-1969. For a search, send $15 per name to:

Graham Hastings
AMA Library & Archives
PO Box 10623
Chicago, IL 60610

American Medical Association will provide current practicing physician profiles by writing to:

A.M.A.
535 N. Dearborn St.
Chicago, IL 60610

Don't forget to check the various Who's Who while in the library.

State Licensing Boards

Many businesses and trades require a license to operate. The license may be from the city, county or state. These records are available to the public. Call your local county government for more information about where the information is currently archived.

Records From

Non-Government

Sources

The Family History Library

The Mormons

The Mormons have amassed the largest collection of genealogically related material in the world. Why?

The Mormons believe in the unification of the family in the hereafter. To obtain that goal, entire families must be "*sealed*" (baptized) together for eternity. They must know who their ancestors were, therefore they have microfilmed the vital records of most of the countries on earth. Communist regimes prior to their downfall allowed the Mormons to microfilm their records. The contracts usually contain a clause that allows the government whose records are being filmed to retain copies of the microfilm.

Records are catalogued and stored in an enormous granite cave in Salt Lake City, Utah. If you are fortunate to do research there, you will find almost every record you can imagine, in their "Library." The one exception is U.S. naturalization papers. "The Library" refers to the archives of the Mormons in Salt Lake City.

Not everyone can go to Utah. Therefore, most cities contain a branch of the Library called Family History Centers (FHC). These Centers are housed in the same building as the church itself and are convenient.

On line: www.Lds.org/family_history/where_is.html

Jewish Support

The Mormon's support the research of everyone's genealogy, and they have microfilmed Jewish as well as Christian records. Access to these records is relatively inexpensive. Over the years a relationship has developed of trust between the FHC and the JGS organizations. Most JGS do not have the facilities to house a large collection of data. Some societies divide their collection with universities that have Judaica libraries. The JGS of Palm Beach County, Florida has a large collection of books. These are housed at Florida Atlantic University's Judaica Library. Other books are housed at the FHC where many of its members do their research.

The Center can be a small office with limited resources or a large research center. Los Angeles contains the largest Family History Center outside of Salt Lake City. The FHC in Los Angeles also contains the library of the Jewish Genealogical Society (JGS) of Los Angeles. The combination makes it a treat for the Jewish researcher. The New York City FHC located at Lincoln Center is another large facility. Its permanent collection is augmented by the JGS (New York).

These centers are staffed by volunteers, some of whom are more experienced than others. Be sure to plan your research goals prior to visiting a center. Be assured that the policy of the FHC is not to proselytize in research areas. More than 95% of their patrons are not Mormon. In twenty-two years of using these centers, I have never once been approached.

And yes, there was a problem a few years back. In every religion there are zealots, and the Mormons certainly have theirs. You may have read about an incident where some members of the Church took it upon themselves to "seal" victims of the Holocaust. A protest was instituted by the Association of Jewish Genealogical Societies, the umbrella organization for the JGS. The uproar by the Jewish community was followed with an apology from the Church.

-37-

Preparing For A Visit

Finding the nearest FHC is easy. Open your Yellow Pages™ to Churches, and find "*The Church of Latter-day Saints*" or "*The Church of Jesus Christ of Latter-day Saints.*" Family History Center's usually have their own telephone listing within that category.

Since these Centers are generally small, check:

- □ Hours of operation
- □ What are the best hours to do research?
- □ Can I make an appointment with a staff person to review my research goals?
- □ Which records are available: on site; special order?
- □ Do you have a computer available to the public?
- □ Do you have to reserve time to use the computer/microfilm reader?
- □ Is time limited on the computer and microfilm reader?
- □ Can I bring a *floppy disk* and download information?
- □ Can I print out information?
- □ Do you have a microfilm reader?

Bring a *Pedigree Chart* with you on your first visit. Also bring a magnifying glass if using the microfilm reader. Some of the data is difficult to read. If your Center is well staffed, the volunteer will be able to guide you to your next step.

International Genealogical Index (IGI)

The IGI is an index to the family trees of approximately 145 million persons(1500-1895). The majority of the trees are of Christian origin.

Ancestral File

If you locate a name in the IGI, continue to the Ancestral File database. The name of the person that donated the information will be listed.

Social Security Death Index

The Social Security Death Index (SSDI) is a list of persons who received Social Security Benefits prior to their death. If used properly, it can yield much information, especially after 1956. Information included in the index are:

- □ Name
- □ Social Security Number
- □ Date of birth
- □ Date of death
- □ Zip code where last benefit check was mailed

This will give you a clue to a next of kin. The next of kin probably lived with or near their children. Check the phone directories for the surname of your ancestor in that zip code county or city.

When searching for the unknown spouse of a deceased, check the SSDI. Limit your search by including the zip code where the last payment was sent to the known spouse. This often yields only one name. This method is especially helpful in locating the spouses of ancestors with common names. The Index is available at the FHC on CD-ROMS (see computer section). You can do a very broad search if you have an unusual name, i.e., Gredinger. For common names like Freedman, Schwartz, etc. try to narrow the search by including the following:

- ☐ Enter the surname of the person you are researching
- ☐ Enter first names if known
- ☐ Enter the date of death if known
- ☐ Enter the date of birth if known
- ☐ Enter state of last known residence if known

Do not check the Soundex search box. You will get too many responses. Within a few seconds you should have the information needed. You may write for a full copy of the SS-5 Application for Social Security card. Proof of death is required for anyone but yourself. A printout of the Social Security information from the index usually is enough. Other forms of proof can be a death certificate or tombstone pictures. Write to:

Office of Central Records Operation
FOIA Workgroup
P.O.Box 1772
300 N. Greene St
Baltimore, MD 21290

If you know the Social Security number, the cost is $7.00, otherwise, the cost is $16.50 (a/o 8/98). The check should be made payable to the Social Security Administration. The index is also available on-line **free** through **www.ancestry.com**. On-line, the information is available through March 1998. See Computer section for more on-line information.

Hamburg Passenger Lists

Many persons leaving Eastern Europe passed through Hamburg on their way to their final destination. After researching Federal records, you might discover that your ancestor's ship left from the Port of Hamburg, during the years 1855-1934. The Hamburg Passenger Indexes and Lists may be another source of information. Many persons saved money by "stopping over" or indirectly coming to the U.S., therefore, check the indirect index first. Written in German, the files are fairly easy to read. Using Naturalization papers as a guide, order the appropriate index reels. Since there are many unindexed years in the U.S. Passenger Arrival Records Indexes, this could be the way to find the ship your relative boarded.

Once you find the name of your ancestor, make a copy of the index card and then order the actual reel that contains the full passenger manifest. You will be able to find the ancestral town and the last residence of that relative. You might find that your ancestor made many stops prior to coming to the U.S.

Hamburg Passenger Lists & Indexes
www.genealogy.com Double click German Emigration to America

Direct Index	1855 -1910
Indirect Index	1854 -1910
surname then chronological	
Direct/Indirect	1911-1914; 1920 -1934
Direct Passenger Lists	1850-1934
Indirect Passenger Lists	1854-1910

World War I Draft Registrations

Other genealogical source of information are the 24.2 million World War I Draft registration cards. Men between the ages of 18-45 were required to register, whether aliens or citizens. Information included:

- ☐ Full names
- ☐ Full date and place of birth
- ☐ Citizenship
- ☐ Occupation
- ☐ Description
- ☐ The name of the wife or nearest relative

The cards are arranged by state, then county or city, then alphabetically. You must know the exact street address or Draft Board for larger cities. This information is also available on line through a subscription to ancestry.com.

The Catalog

This CD-ROM contains the entire holdings of the Library in Salt Lake City. Included are descriptions of the 1.6 million microfilm reels and 200,000 books. Call numbers are included to enable you to order these books and microfilm.

Locality Search

You are interested in finding any records about the city where your ancestors lived. A Locality Search helps you find what records are available. You inquire whether there are records for the Emigration or Immigration from Philadelphia, or Poland. Remember, Jews are usually listed under a sub-category of "Minorities."

Military Death Index

This Index covers those persons killed in the Korean Conflict and the Viet Nam War.

Clues From Tombstones

The traditional Jewish tombstone contains a wealth of information. Jewish people bury their dead as quickly as possible. The tombstone that follows is typical. The new practice of only inscribing only the decedent's name and date of death on the foot stone is as yet not widespread. Analyze the following tombstone. The full Hebrew name of the decedent, including the father's Hebrew name appears on the tombstone. Information

about the individual, i.e. father, brother. First names of
the decedent's date of death and age.

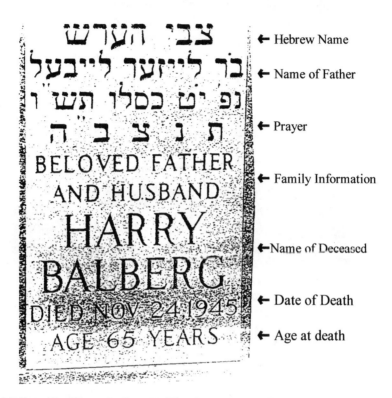

← Hebrew Name

← Name of Father

← Prayer

← Family Information

←Name of Deceased

← Date of Death

← Age at death

Guidelines for Translating the Tombstone Inscription

First Line:

TOP: Here is interned . . . פב

Second Line:

Deceased Hebrew name and that of their Parent
i.e., *Gadalia Isaac* **bar** Reb Manasha

Reb(Mister) = ר   Bar (son of) = בר

Bat (daughter of) = בט

The words following Bar or Bat (Bas) are The words before it is the Hebrew/Yiddish names of the deceased followed by the name of the parent.

Third and Fourth Lines:
May his/her soul be bound up in the bonds of eternal life. . . . תנצב"ה

You need only translate the second line to obtain the Hebrew name of the deceased and that of their parent.

From the tombstone above you can determine that Isaac was married and had living children at the time of his death. The date of his death and his age, 80, are listed. Rose is on the same family tombstone. The birth information determines that she is probably Isaac's wife. Note that Jack's father's Hebrew name is listed as Gadalia Isaac. Jack therefore is the son of Isaac.

Check the general area of burial for other persons with the same name. Inquire at the cemetery office for the names of other relatives. Most cemeteries are computerized and can easily check burial records. Limit your inquiries to five names.

While in the cemetery office, request the name of the person responsible for your family's grave site. This can be someone from the *landsmanshaften* organization and/or a relative. Occasionally you will find a cemetery that will not disclose this information. When that happens, hand them a pre-written letter, explaining why you are contacting the responsible person. You should include your return address on the envelope with the notation *"forwarding and address correction guaranteed."* This is especially important when dealing with older tombstones as the contact person may also have died. Include a self addressed stamped envelope. Use the form below to record information found at a grave site.

Extracts From Tombstone

Here lies _____
    Son ❑   Daughter ❑ of _____
    Wife ❑   Husband ❑ Grandmother ❑   Grandfather ❑
    Other:_____
Born: _____
Died: _____
Age: _____
Cemetery: _____
Plot Location: _____
Next of Kin: _____
Other Relatives in Same Cemetery

You learned that Ashkenazi Jews name a child after a deceased relative. The Hebrew/Yiddish name is always sons/daughter of . . . It is easier to take a picture of all the tombstones in a family plot and translate them later. You can also use the tombstone pictures as a form of proof of death when requesting information from archives. Always have extra film and batteries. You do not want to have gone all the way out to a cemetery only to find that the camera does not work.

You have just discovered another generation. This is confirmation of other information you have gathered. You may order the death record since you now have the exact date of death. Older tombstones may be completely in Hebrew.

Have a person fluent in Hebrew translate the stone for you or use the guide below. There is a pattern to all tombstones. The following are some of the more common words used.

Husband . . . כע'   Wife . . . א ש ה

Father . . . א ב'   Mother . . . א מ'

Brother . . . א ח'   Sister . . . א ת ו ת

Born . . . נ ו ל ד (ה)   Day . . . ו ס'

This Month . . . ח ד ש   Died . . . נ פ ט ר(ה)

Son of . . . ב ר   Daughter of . . . ב ט

Mr. (Reb) . . . ר'

Many letters are phonetically interchangeable. They include:

B and P	D and T	F, Ph, and V
I and Y	K and G	M and N
P and B	V and W	S and Z

Most tombstones contain relief drawings. These can be clues to the identity, occupation or character of the deceased. Refer to the examples below.

A tombstone with hands spread indicates the individual was a Kohen (priest), a male descent of Aaron The Kohanim raise their hands to give blessings.

A basin and pitcher appear on the graves of Levites. They are the descendants of the tribe of Levi. They are responsible for washing the priests (Kohanim).

The next example shows a pair of scissors. We know the deceased was a tailor.

A Lion holding a trumpet suggests the name Yehudah or Leib. The trumpet indicates his entry into heaven. The lion is also used to signify the tribe of Judah.

Candelabra's often adorn the graves of women, reflecting the duty of women to light candles.

A rabbi or scholar might have the tombstone below.

Dates on a tombstone are shortened to the last three numbers. i.e. 5758 becomes 758. To arrive at the Common Era year use the formula of: the number, i.e. 758 + *1240* = 1998. Some older tombstones list the date of death in Hebrew.

The Hebrew Calendar

The Hebrew Calendar is a lunar calendar consisting of 354 days, divided into twelve months. An extra month (Adar II) is added seven times during a nineteen-year cycle.

The Jewish year begins in the spring with Nisan (March-April) and ends with Adar (February-March). Rosh Hashana occurs in Tishri, the seventh month and marks the Creation. Older Jews remember the date of an *event* by the holiday it was near. As an example: "Papa always said he was born during Chanukah." Ashkenazi tradition restricts celebrations during the period beginning the second night of *Passover* and ending on *Shavuot*. During the Middle Ages, pogroms took place during this time, hence no public gatherings such as weddings.

Newspaper Obituaries and Ads

Knowing the date of death makes it easier to search the obituary "ads." Ads are placed by the undertaker. Your local research library has back issues of various newspapers available on microfilm. The obituary notice or article will list the names of the surviving family members. Pre-1970 notices sometimes included the address of the *Shiva*. Remember to check defunct newspaper morgues as well. The New York Public Library, Fifth Avenue and Forty-Second Street has the largest collection of newspapers on microfilm.

① Make lists of all persons to be researched and their approximate date of death.

② Check your local library for *The New York Times Obituary Index* if your relative was prominent.

③ Order microfilm for specific city newspapers from your library.

④ Check the entire week that your relative died for the undertaker's notice (ad).

⑤ If the newspaper is not on microfilm, write to the newspaper requesting a search of their morgue. Limit your request and provide a date of death. Many newspapers are "on-line" i.e. nytimes.com

City Directories

Prior to the printing of telephone books, residents of a town or city were recorded in *City Directories*. A City Directory lists the name, occupation, work and home address of individuals. You need to know the exact address of a person in order to search non-indexed census schedules. Many state census schedules as well as the Federal 1910 Census fall into this category. City Directories then become invaluable tools.

A method for narrowing the search of death or immigration records would include checking these directories. Many times the letter *w* appeared after a name in the directory. This would indicate the *widow* of the original listed person.

Refer back to the Questionnaire in Chapter 2. Notice that specific years were listed. These are the dates of state and federal census schedules. If your relative was engaged in either a business or profession, check the advertisements in the directories for clues.

① Find the city directories for the earliest year your relative resided in that city.

② Search the key census years (and the year before and after). Record the address for each person on a separate address directory form found in the appendix.

Landsmanshaften Organizations

You want to confirm the name of the town your immigrant ancestor emigrated from. The best sources for obtaining this information are:

Census records	Cemetery records
Vital records	Oral testimony of relatives

Assume you know the name of the town. The immigrant upon arriving in the United States lived with or near relatives. If the immigrant did not have American relatives, he would live with other persons that originated from the same town or country. The *Landsmanshaften* helped the immigrant assimilate into their new American life. Many of the organizations provided financial and medical services. At one time more than six hundred thousand Jews lived on the Lower East Side of New York. There were more than three hundred landsmanshaften Shuls (small prayer houses), often consisting of a large room or storefront.

The Landsmanshaften distributed relief payments for the *landslayt* (residents from the same towns) both in Europe and in the United States. Burial was arranged for its members. The Society records were often in Yiddish.

The transcript of meeting minutes can often lead to information. A typical entry might include: "Our member Moshe Friedmann's son Hymie was married Sunday. Isidore Leibowitz, on behalf of the organization, gave the couple a wedding present of $10." Similar entries can be found for gifts in honor of a birth. Baskets of fruit were sent upon a death. The reports of a doctor being sent to visit a member are often entered. Purchases of burial plot, and loans can be found in the minutes of meetings.

Check the notices and/or an advertisement in the remembrance journals. You may find a picture of your ancestor.

Locating the Records of a Landsmanshaften

The largest repository of Landsmanshaften records is at YIVO in New York (see Judaica Archives). If you are unable to visit YIVO, check other archives for Memorial books of your town. Many of these organizations are still active in Israel. Contact:

Association of Polish Jews in Israel
158 Dizzengof St
63461 Tel Aviv, Israel
972-3-522-5078; fax 972-3-523-6684

Ask for name and address of Chairman for your town.

Lower East Side Tenement Museum

While Jews have been in the U.S. prior to the Revolutionary War, the first totally Jewish neighborhood appeared in the 1870's at the corner of Bayard and Mott Streets. While visiting New York City, you can go to 97 Orchard Street, Manhattan, the home of the Lower East Side Tenement Museum. The insight into the life for the immigrant (1880-1920) is authentic. A published list of names and dates of persons that lived at that address has been compiled.

Synagogue Records

From your questionnaire you have determined your family was active in a synagogue. Yeshiva University Archive (NY) houses the records of the Orthodox movement while the Jewish Theological Seminary (NY) has Conservative congregational records and some Orthodox records. The. Hebrew Union College in Cincinnati houses the records for the Reform movement.

Check if the synagogue still exists at the same location. If the synagogue is still in existence contact the office and inquire whether your family records (Bris, Bar/bat Mitzvah, wedding) records are still available at that location. Inquire if Synagogue anniversary journals are available. They often contain pictures and information about persons.

Yahrzeit (the yearly anniversary of a person's death) memorial plaques for family members are another source of information. Ask if any of your relatives donated money for one. Request a picture of the plaque. The plaque lists the date of death and the full Hebrew name of the deceased.

←Date of Death
←Hebrew Name

Send a donation to cover expenses.

Judaic Libraries & Archives

> Libraries can be a great source for genealogical secondary information. Check your local library for printed histories of the towns and cities you are researching. There may be a reference to your relative.
>
> Look for the Who's Who for 19xx to find a biography of an individual. Locate the Encyclopedia Judaica, preferably the 1897 edition. It lists many of the European shtetls.
>
> Contact or visit a Judaica library. A list appears in "Where to write for what." Do not ask the librarian or archivist to do research for you unless you are prepared to pay for it.

Jewish Genealogical Societies

> There are more than 75 Jewish Genealogical Societies (JGS) worldwide. Joining a JGS will enable you to interact with persons of similar interests. Most JGS meet regularly and publish newsletters. A list of these groups is provided in the chapter JGS, SIG, and Historical Associations.

SIG

> In addition to the local JGS, there are "Special Interest Groups" (SIG). A SIG is an organization that specializes in one geographic region or country. Many times it covers two countries, but one historical *gubernia* (province).

Historical Societies

> Historical societies can be of great help to the family historian. Often they have secondary sources that can

lead the researcher to the primary source being sought. Write to a Jewish or secular Historical society in the city your ancestor lived. They should have a newspaper collection. If you know the date of death for a relation, ask the librarian to examine the newspapers for that time period and send you the obituary notice. Write and ask what information they have that may be of help to you. Be specific in your request. Remember the SASE.

*S*tate and Local

Government Records

Vital Records

*V*ital Records consist of those documents that record the *events* in a persons life. An official record should be available for every birth, marriage, divorce and death. You must know the county and city/town where the event took place. Some state indexes i.e. California list events that occurred during a specified time for the entire state. Specifically request a copy of the original records, not a certificate. The record contains all the information available from the file, while the certificate "certifies" the information contained is correct. Include as many of the following facts about the person whose record you are requesting for optimum results:

- ☐ Full name of the individual
- ☐ Fathers' name
- ☐ Birth name of mother
- ☐ Month, Day and Year of event
- ☐ Place of birth, town and county
- ☐ Your relationship to the person
- ☐ Sign a hyphenated name,
      i.e. Edward Balberg-Grediger

When the exact date of an event is not provided, a search fee may be charged.

Some states do not honor requests for information when the stated purpose is "genealogical research." Word your request appropriately in those states.

Birth Records

A Birth Register records:

- ☐ Date of birth,
- ☐ Location of that birth
- ☐ Names and full the address of the parents
- ☐ Occupation of parents'
- ☐ Infant's official name

The record typically contains the place of birth of the parents and the age of both parents. Birth records less than 72 years old are customarily available only to the named individual.

Before 1920 most births took place in the home, and the record of these births was filed by the mid-wife. Often these records were delayed, sometimes a week, sometimes longer. These are known as *delayed birth records*. The example above is from 1943, forty years after the birth of the child. The birth certificate relies on secondary sources for its information. Treat it accordingly.

A death certificate or tombstone photograph are acceptable forms of proof of death when requesting recent birth records.

Death Records

Death Records are documents in which a decedent's family member or friend has provided the biographical information. The resulting information is based on how much that person knew about the deceased background.

Frequently you will find that a person died in one state or city, and is buried in another. This is not unusual, especially for retired Sunbelt residents, and for persons that reside close to a state border. The death records will be found in both states, the state of death and the state of burial.

Jewish Genetic Diseases

If your ancestor had a genetic disease, you should note this in their file. Their descendants should be aware of what treatments they can avail themselves of in relation to the ailment. See the Appendix for a list of a few of the many Jewish diseases and disorders.

Reference Guide

The booklet *"Where to Write for Vital Records"* (DHHS # PHS 93-1142) is published by the U.S. Department of Health and Human Services. The booklet contains the addresses and fee structure for vital records for every state. Included in this publication are agencies that recorded events outside the continental United States for American citizens. You may purchase this publication by writing to:

U.S. Government Printing Office
Superintendent of Documents
SSOP
Washington, D.C. 20402-9328

A list of selected addresses of state vital record offices appears in "Where to Write."

Marriage Records

After the marriage, an officiant signs and submits a marriage record to the local governing body. The marriage record contains:

- □ Names of bride and groom,
- □ Addresses prior to the marriage
- □ Previous marital status
- □ Names of parents
- □ Witnesses to the marriage
- □ Birthplaces of the bridal couple
- □ Location of marriage ceremony

Most archives have indexes to these marriages. These indexes are commonly referred to as:

General Index to marriages (year) (locality).
Brides Index to marriages (birth surname of the bride).
Grooms Index to marriages (a surname index).

Brides Index to marriages (birth surname of the bride). *Grooms* Index to marriages (a surname index).

If you know the groom's name, i.e. Harry Cohen and the bride's birth name, i.e. Esther Cackin, you should check the bride's index first, narrowing down the possible marriages to Harry Cohen. If the groom has the unusual name, the reverse would be true.

Compare the following Marriage Record with the Certificate of Marriage on page 63. Note how much more information you receive in the Marriage Record versus the Certificate.

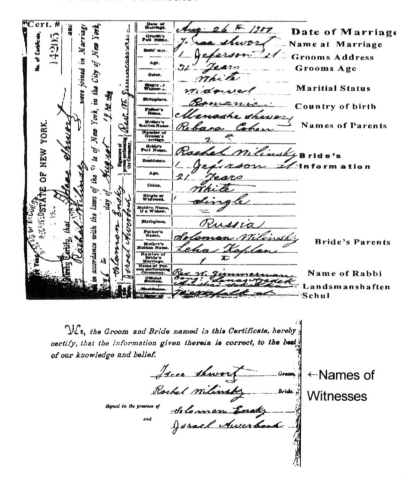

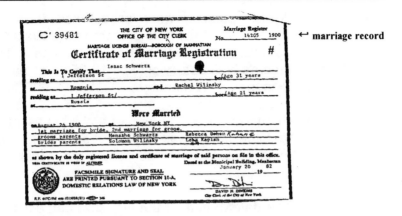

← marriage record

Divorce Records

Divorce records are public records available with great limitations. They are located at the county courthouse where the divorce occurred. The place of marital residence generally establishes the place of divorce or annulment. Older divorce are available through the Family History Centers. When records are available they include the following:

- ▫ Names of husband and wife.
- ▫ Date of divorce or annulment.
- ▫ Place of divorce or annulment.
- ▫ Type of final decree.

Estimating the Ages of Your Ancestors

While researching records you will often combine information from different sources. You may have to approximate the ages of your ancestors. Birth dates that appear in Census records can be *"interpretive."* Many individuals' ages varied from document to document by as much as ten years. When applying for Social Security individuals became older, where as when they applied for marriage applications and census records they became younger.

> ❑ Jewish persons were encouraged to marry young. Using the date of marriage subtract 16-25 years to estimate the bride's age. The groom's birth date would be 18-25 years earlier than that of his marriage.
>
> ❑ Use the date of the birth of a child to estimate that the father was 16-45 years older. The mother could be 16-38 years older than the child.
>
> ❑ The date of birth of the first child can estimate the date a marriage occurred. Subtract ten to eighteen months prior to the birth.
>
> ❑ Look at Hebrew names of cousins to estimate the date of death of the person they were named for.
>
> ❑ Each generation is calculated to be twenty - five years.

Voter Registration

The Registrar of Voters has additional information about your ancestor. Voter's registration forms are public records. A copy of the proof of citizenship is required to be eligible to vote. This usually will be their Certificate of Naturalization for a foreign born citizen or the birth record for a native born citizen.

Provide the Registrar of Elections with the full name, address (including county) of your relative. Use the date of a presidential election to achieve optimum results. In earlier years, voters had to register before each election.

Probate

Probate records are a great source for the genealogist. Contained in the probate records you will find:

- □ Date of Death (Death Certificate/Record)
- □ Date and location of burial
- □ Will
- □ Names and addresses of **all** direct descendants
- □ Names and addresses of all beneficiaries and heirs
- □ Social Security numbers of beneficiaries (recent documents)
- □ Description of relationships between those eligible to inherit and deceased
- □ Listing of property owned at time of death

A will is a public legal document containing the statement of a person's wishes regarding the disposal of his property after death. When a will is probated, proof of the validity of the will is required.

If the deceased owned any property, i.e. a house, no matter how heavy mortgaged, the estate would be eligible for probate. In the event of a beneficiary's death, proof of that death will be documented. Probate records are located at the **County Courthouse of the legal residence** of that individual, not necessarily where they lived or died.

- □ Determine the county of official residence
- □ Go to county courthouse
- □ Request *Index to Administrations and Estates*

Make sure you have picture identification with you, as proof of your identity may be requested. The index is generally arranged by year, then surnames. Note the file number.

Application: Surrogate's Court-NY County

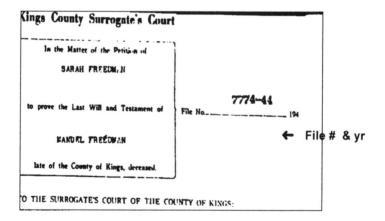

The second page of the Petition for Probate lists the names of heirs and their relationship to the deceased. You will also find the address of the heirs at the time of filing. Sometimes citizenship status is included. Even when a will is filed, persons who would inherit if there was not a will (*intestate*) are listed. In the next example, military rank and units are noted for both Aaron and Abraham Freedman.

NAME	OR INTEREST	ADDRESS	CITIZENSHIP
Irving Bernard Freedman	Son	1736 Prospect Place, Brooklyn, New York.	U.S.A.
Pauline Siegel	Daughter	977 Herkimer Street, Brooklyn, New York.	U.S.A.
Hyman Freedman	Son	2016 Union Street, Brooklyn, New York	U.S.A.
Mrs. Mollie Becker	Daughter	2041 Pacific Street, Brooklyn, New York	U.S.A.
Pfc. Abraham Freedman	Son	Co.5,80th-CML-Bn. N.T.Z.D. Camp Swift, Texas.	U.S.A.
Aaron Freedman,SK3C	Son	Dist. officer.AMP Training Corp., Camp Bradford, N.C.B., Norfolk, Virginia.	
Ida Freedman	Daughter	977 Herkimer St., Brooklyn, New York.	U.S.A.
SARAH FREEDMAN	WIDOW	977 HERKIMER ST. BROOKLYN N.Y.	RUSSIA

← military rank

In the next example the last known address of the beneficiaries is listed. The minor children's relationships to the deceased are listed as well.

Name & Address	Relationship	Devise or Other Interest or Nature of Fiduciary Status
Laura Werstein 102-25 67th Drive Queens, New York 11375	Sister	Personal property and one-half (1/2) of residuary estate; Co-Executor
Alfred Cohen 2 Padot Lane Yonkers, New York	Nephew	None
Ruth Herman 2135 Wallace Ave. Bronx, New York 10462	Niece	Seven percent (7%) of residuary estate
Laura Pine 2076 Wallace Ave. Bronx, New York 10462	Niece	Twelve percent (12%) of residuary estate
Samuel Cohen 2135 Wallace Ave. Bronx, New York 10462	Nephew	Seven percent (7%) of residuary estate
Merle Goldstein 116? Village Drive Hauppauge, New York 11787	Grandniece	None
Robert L. Fromer 30 Lighthouse Road Kings Point, New York 11024	None	Co-Executor

Other information found in probate records can be of real property owned by the deceased, even if the property is heavily mortgaged..

The decedent at the time of his death was the owner in fee simple of a house and lot known as 977 Herkimer Street, in the Borough of Brooklyn, City of New York.

The property is situated on the northerly side of Herkimer Street, distant 165 feet easterly from the corner of Ralph Avenue and Herkimer Street, and the same is twenty feet wide and 100 feet deep on the inside.

On said lot is situated a two-family building over thirty years old which has general improvements. One apartment is rented for $28.00 monthly and the true rental value of the entire building is about $60.00 per month.

The property was purchased by Manuel Freedman, the deceased, on May 17, 1923 and the deed to same is recorded in Liber 4245, page 538 of Conveyances in the Register's Office in the County of Kings, City of New York, on May 25, 1923. The said house and lot was assessed for the year 1943-1944 at .... $ 4,000.00
True value in 1944 - $4,000.00.

The said property was at the time of the death of the decedent and still is covered by a mortgage in the sum of $1,350.00 bearing interest at the rate of 4½ per cent per annum and held by the Manufacturer's Trust Co of New York City 1,350.00

This parcel of real estate is known as lot 62 in block 1548 of Section 6 in the Register's Office of the County of Kings, City of New York. Equity in house - 2,650.00

Federal Records

Research

T his chapter teaches you how to research Federal Records properly including:

☐ Population Censuses
☐ Naturalization Papers
☐ Passenger Arrival Records

National Archives

The U.S. National Archives in Washington, D.C. is the primary source for U.S. Federal Census Records Passenger Lists, Military Records, and some Naturalization records.

Census Records are valuable resources, and are very easy to use. The U.S. Federal Census has been taken every ten years, since 1790. The 1920 Census is the most recent publicly available. Most census records have been indexed:

Table of Census Records

1790-1870	Head of household
1880	Complete Soundex for each state. Partial indexes for all states. Includes only households with children under aged 10.
1890	Census destroyed in a fire, thus no index.
1900	Complete Soundex for each state.
1910	Partial Soundex for 21 states (most in the South and West): AL, AR, CA, FL, **GA**, IL, KS, KY, LA, **MI**, MS, MO, NC, **OH**, OK, **PA**, SC, TN, TX, VA, WV.
1920	Complete Soundex for each state

There is a 72-year privacy rule for census records. Records 1930 and later are restricted to the persons in the record itself or their heirs.

Write to:

> Bureau of the Census
> Personal Census Service Branch
> P.O. Box 1545
> Jeffersonville, IN 47130
> (812)288- 3300

A death certificate or signature of the individual the information is about is required. A minimum search fee is $40 per person per year searched is imposed.

Regional Archives

In addition to the main archive in Washington, the National Archives maintains thirteen Regional Archives. Each archive will have on microfilm:

- All Census Indexes and Schedules 1790-1920
- Military Records
- Passenger Lists for that region
- Local Federal records, including Federal Court Naturalization Records for that Region

The National Archives and its branches are open to the public and available for use free of charge. Microfilms are in open cabinets, and the staff is helpful and knowledgeable. Most of the Archives microfilms are available through the FHC. (See Where to Write)

Soundex

The records are voluminous therefore, how do you tackle this job when you are not sure of the correct spelling of your ancestors name? The answer is Soundex, a system that reduces surnames to a mathematical formula based on the way a name sounds rather than the way it is spelled.

No matter how much information you already know, using Soundex will expedite finding the exact page and line number in the document you are searching. i.e. If you know the name of the ship, date and port of arrival, use the Soundex anyway to direct you to the exact page and line number in the document. Reading faded, often illegible handwritten pages and trying to locate an entry can be tedious. These records were indexed as a project of the WPA (Works Progress (Projects) Administration).

Determining a surname's code:

Step 1:

- ☐ Write the surname you are coding in the following box. Place the first letter of the surname in box 1, second letters in box 2, etc.

- ☐ Following the example below crossing out all vowels unless the vowel is the first letter of the surname.
- ☐ Cross out the letter's W, Y, and H unless they are the first letter of the surname.

Double Letters:

- ☐ If your surname has any double letters, eliminate the second letter, i.e., FF, LL, RR

    M ~~O~~ R ~~R~~ ~~I~~ S = M 620

- ☐ When the surname has letters side by side and are the same Soundex number, they are treated as the same letter. i.e. ck, sk, sc

- ☐ An exception to the rules occurs in certain names i.e. Schwartz, Schuster etc. The first and second letters have the same combined sound.

    S ~~CH~~ W A R T Z = S 632
    S ~~CH~~ U S T E R   = S 236

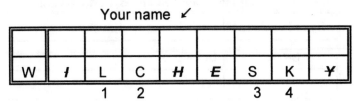

Your name ✓

W	*I*	L	C	*H*	*E*	S	K	*Y*

1   2   3   4

Step 2:

     □   Enter the first four (4) letters of your name that were not eliminated in step 2 to the box below.

Your name ✓

W	L	C	S	First 4 Letters ->				
W	4	2	2	<-SOUNDEX CODE->				

Box 1 2 3 4

Step 4:

> **Soundex Coding Guide**
>
> 1 = **B P F V**
> 2 = **C S K G J Q X Z**
> 3 = **D, T**
> 4 = **L**
> 5 = **M, N**
> 6 = **R**

     □   Using the *Soundex Coding Guide* insert the appropriate numerals in boxes 2, 3 and 4.

     □   If the name doesn't contain enough letters, add zeros (0) to fill blank boxes.   i.e.Kahn = K-500

Many state Driver's Licenses use the Soundex code. Check yours and find the Soundex Code.

Internet users can check soundex codes by going to: **www.jewishgen.org/jossound.htm**

Sample User's Soundex Coding Table

Soundex Code	Surname
S-632	Schwartz

Census Records

Census schedules are readily available and contain a wealth of information for the family historian/genealogist. The Census was authorized under an Act of Congress in 1790 and the First Population Schedule was taken that August. Population Censuses are taken every ten years.

Between 1830 and 1900 the date for the census count was June 1. The date was changed in 1910 to April 15 while the 1930 through 1990 census' were conducted April 1. The 1920 (Fourteenth Census) took place January 1 and is the last census available to the public at this time.

The 1910 census is difficult to use because it does not have Soundex (See page 70 for your state). You must know the exact address and dates of residence to convert addresses to enumeration districts.[1] Many enumeration districts consisted of one apartment building (tenement). Use the 1880, 1900 or 1920 Census' instead.

Census research is fairly easy but you must know the state your relative resided in and preferably the city. If Grandpa Hy lived in Boston in May, 1900 but moved to New York in June, he will not be found in the

---

[1]*Enumeration district* - area allocated to one census taker

The Card INDEX includes many important items. Always note the County, Enumeration District (E.D.), Sheet number and Line number. Citizenship status of all persons is listed.

Key to the abbreviations under citizenship columns:

A	= Alien
Pa	= Papers Filed (Petition)
Na	= Naturalized
NR	= Not Relevant
C	= Citizen

The 1920 Census

The 1920 Census eliminated the questions of length of marriage and number of children. It added more importantly for genealogists:

□ Year of Naturalization

The enumerators were instructed to report the province or city of birth of all persons born in Austria-Hungary, Germany, Russia or Turkey. Even if they were American born, when their parents were born in the above countries, they were supposed to list that as well. Unfortunately, this was often not true.

A word of caution: remember that no proof was required of persons with their answers to the census recorder. If grandma told grandpa she was born in 1891, she was not ready to tell the enumerator that she really was born in 1888. Check the name of the enumerator. Giuseppe Sanchez interviewing Yiddish speaking Isaac Schwartz can lead to many inconsistencies. The enumerator was not allowed to ask for the spelling of surnames, so this information is also interpretive.
Consider *all* possible spelling variations of the name. Capital T, L, and S can easily be interchanged. E and I can also be. Angle, Engle, Ingle, Yingle. With Soundex coding, remember, the first letter is very important.

Exercise:

Locate records for Mendel Schwartz of New York.

Step 1.

Soundex the name Schwartz and enter it in the box below.

S	C	H	W	A	R	T	Z

Step 2.

Consult the *Catalogue of the 1920 Federal Population Census Microfilm.* Turn to the heading for the applicable state and note the Microfilm Series Number. i.e. New York = M 1578

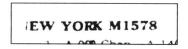

Step 3.

Find the Soundex heading for Schwartz (S-632). The first column indicates reel number. You will note that code S-632 appears in two reel numbers.781 and 782. Using the first name Mendel, the record reel number is 781 .

```
769.  S-540 S.--S-545 Myer
770.  S-545 N. Allen--S-550 Josefine
771.  S-550 Joseph---S-552 Ezra
772.  S-552 F. Howard--S-556 William
773.  S-560 (N.R.)--S-561 Kattie
774.  S-561 Lon--S-600 Dwight
775.  S-600 E.--S-600 Vivian
776.  S-600 W.B.--S-615 Gustave
777.  S-615 Hanna M.--S-620 Iva L.
778.  S-620 J.--S-625 Fritz M.
779.  S-625 Gabriel--S-630 Zula E.
780.  S-631 Abe--S-632 Lyulph G.
781.  S-632 M.--S-635 Lydia
782.  S-635 Mabel--S-642 Gustave
783.  S-642 H. Olay---S-652 Ruple
784.  S-652 Ladinna---S-656 Dorothy
785.  S-656 Earl R.---T-115 William
786.  T-120 (N.R.)--T-150 Izzy
```

Step 4.

Go to the cabinet containing M 1578, then the drawer containing reel 781. Remove the box with the reel of microfilm.

Step 5.

At the microfilm reader transcribe or photocopy the index, making note of the County, Enumeration District, Sheet and Line #. (See page 75)

Census Schedule

You are ready to search for the copy of the actual census. Assume that in your research you found your Mendel Schwartz living in New York County (Manhattan), E.D. 215, page 5 line 6

Step 1.

Once again consult the *Catalogue of the 1920 Federal Population Census Microfilm*. This time turn to the state heading of New York and note the microfilm series **T 625**. This begins on page 51.

1920 CENSUS SCHEDULES
T625   2,076 rolls

Step 2.

Using the information obtained on the index card, turn to the page that lists the microfilm reels from the State of New York. Next check for the County, New York (Manhattan). Go to ED # 215. Note the reel number is 1188.

1185. New York Co., Manhattan Borough (EDs 66-106).

1186. New York Co., Manhattan Borough (EDs 107-149).

1187. New York Co., Manhattan Borough (EDs 150-186).

➤ 1188. New York Co., Manhattan Borough (EDs 187-226).

1189. New York Co., Manhattan Borough (EDs 227-265).

1190. New York Co., Manhattan Borough (EDs 266-306).

1191. New York Co., Manhattan Borough (EDs 307-312 and 314

Step 3.

At your research facility find the microfilm cabinet that contains T 625, then open the drawer containing reel number 1188.

Step 4.

On the microfilm reel, go directly to E.D. 215, Sheet 5, Line 6. You will find Mendel and his family.

Step 5.

Photocopy or transcribe pertinent information.

Note: Check other inhabitants of area for possible relatives.

Census Research Worksheet

Soundex	Name	Census Year	Index Reel		Census Reel		ED County	Sheet #	Line #
S-632	Mendel Schwartz	1920	M 1578	781	T 625	1189	215	5	6

Naturalization Records

Naturalization is the process by which an alien (immigrant) becomes a citizen of the United States. Prior to 1906, the immigrant could file their application for citizenship at either a state, county or federal court. In 1906, the federal government formed the Immigration and Naturalization Service (INS) centralizing the process.

The outbreak of World War I (1914-1918) caused many immigrants to file a *Declaration of Intention* also know as "First Papers." This document was valid for only seven years. An additional reason for the rush for naturalization at this time was a change in the law. After 1922, the applicant' wife and children over eighteen years of age would no longer automatically become citizens based on their father's naturalization. They would have to file their own papers.

U. S. DEPARTMENT OF LABOR
NATURALIZATION SERVICE

TRIPLICATE

UNITED STATES OF AMERICA

DECLARATION OF INTENTION

Invalid for all purposes seven years after the date hereof

of New York,
rict of New York, } ss.

In the District Court of the United States.

Manuel Freedman, aged 41 years,

Foreman, do declare on oath that my person

s: Color white, complexion fair, height 5 feet 6 inches,

120 pounds, color of hair brown, color of eyes gray

Last residence → distinctive marks none

n Grodna, Russia,

5th day of March, anno Domini 1881; I now reside
246 Clinton St.,
(Give number and street.)
, New York City, N. Y.

Arrival → into the United States of America from St. John,

By Railroad ; my last
(If the alien arrival otherwise than by vessel, the character or name of transportation company should be given.)
ce was Canada ; I am married; the name
s Sarah ; she was born at Russia,
es at with me,

fide intention to renounce forever all allegiance and fidelity to any foreign
nce, state, or sovereignty, and particularly to of whom I am now a subject;

the port of N.Y. , in the
N.Y. , on or about the 23rd day

nc. , anno Domini 1 903 I am not an anarchist; I am not a
believer in the practice of polygamy; and it is my intention in good faith
zen of the United States of America and to permanently reside therein:
GOD.

Manuel Freedman
(Original signature of declarant.)

Subscribed and sworn to before me in the office of the Clerk of said Court

at New York City, N. Y., this 3 day of July
anno Domini 19 22.

Deputy Clerk of the District Court of the United States.

The above document lists the name of the applicant, occupation, physical description, the name of the wife, dates of arrival in the United States and the method of entering the United States. It also contains the country to which they owed allegiance and the **exact date of birth** of the applicant. Note in this example, the immigrant arrived in the United States by rail from St. John. This was the train depot for immigrants that arrived at the Canadian Port of Halifax. The alien's current address is also declared. Another requirement was that the immigrant had resided continuously in the United States for a minimum of one year.

The next papers filed was called the Petition for Naturalization, also known as the "Second Papers." A requirement to be eligible for citizenship was having resided in the country continuously for five years. Besides the information from the Declaration of Intention, the applicant's wife's information is included. You will have the "reported" birth dates for the immigrant and his wife. In addition, all children of the applicant are listed, their birth dates and places of birth.

Tip:

Photocopy the *Affidavits of Witnesses*. A requirement to be a witness was U.S. citizenship and knowledge of the applicant's character. Witnesses were relatives, close friends or landsmen. If it turns out the witness was a relative, check their citizenship papers and confirm the connection. In the previous Anna Cohen and Isidore Leon were both cousins of Isaac. The address listed for Anna and Isidore were their addresses in 1913.

Petition Number →

The *Certificate of Naturalization* is the last document, and the one immigrant gets to keep. This has the least information for the genealogist.

If you are lucky and have found a Certificate of Naturalization, you will have the Petition Number for the previous applications of citizenship.

How to find Naturalization Records

Step 1.

Check the 1920 Census. Was your ancestor a citizen at that time? If yes, check 1900 Census. This will enable you to focus in on a time span of citizenship.

Step 2.

Copy the Soundex Code for all persons being researched.

Step 3.

Use the Soundex to find Index to Naturalization papers 1906-1956.

☐ Record:
☐ Date of Naturalization
☐ Volume
☐ Page and Record Number

Table for Naturalization Research

Soundex #	Name	Date	Vol #	Pg #	Record #	Misc. Information

Step 4.

Either order from the FHC the microfilm that lists your ancestor or visit the nearest National Archive branch to research the papers.

Passenger Arrival Records

Passenger Arrival Records (manifests)are records that the personnel aboard a ship prepared about alien (non-citizen) passengers prior to their disembarkation.

Contrary to belief, the official at "Ellis Island" did not change the immigrant's name!

There has never been even one case of a name changed by the American official reported. This is simply a story that took on a life of its own and is now believed as fact by almost everyone. Genealogical information includes:

- □ Name of Ship
- □ Dates of departure and arrival
- □ Port sailed from
- □ Passenger's name, age and marital status
- □ Occupation
- □ Nationality - last place of residence
- □ Final destination
- □ Name and relationship of relative sponsor
- □ Address of that relative

This is the document that will start you on your research overseas. It is the very first document your ancestor completed after leaving Europe.

Step 1

Decide which Ports of Arrival records to research based on your research. i.e .Census, Naturalization records.

Step 2

Keep a permanent **Soundex** chart of all passengers' names you plan to research.

Step 3

Following the same procedure that you used in researching Census Records, consult *Immigrant & Passenger Arrival Publication*, Index section. Each port of entry is listed separately.

Step 4

Note record group number (i.e., T 519) and reel number.

Step 5

Using a microfilm reader, note all information on microfilm **Index Card,** especially **Volume, Page and Line number.**

Step 6

Consult again the *Immigrant & Passenger Arrival Publication*.

Step 7

Check Passenger List. Note **Record** and **Reel** number.

Step 8

Advance a microfilm reader until you find the Soundex number appearing on the upper left hand corner.

Step 9

Go to first letter of the given name. Check **all** possible versions of name-- Hymie, Hyman, Chaim, Charles etc.

Happy hunting!

TIP:

You may be looking for a Max Wolfe, from Russia who visited the United States but returned to Europe. Assume Max visited N.Y. between 1905 and 1920. Naturalization and Census research would not be helpful, as he did not stay and become a citizen. You will be doing a blind index search.

Looking through index cards will only tell you that hundreds of Max Wolfe's arrived at the Port of NY between 1902 and 1920. After 1902, the year was no longer included on the index card, only the Volume Number of the book the *record of arrival* appeared in.

Brian Andersson wrote *"Andersson's Guide to Those Numbers"* in which he cross-referenced for the port of New York: the year of arrival and volume numbers to the National Archives reel numbers. Below is his chart.

Andersson's Chart

Year	Volume #	Nat'l Archives Reel #
1902	485-550	288 - 315
1903	551-792	316- 425
1904	793-1064	425 - 525
1905	1065-1416	525-625
1906	1417-1848	626-815
1907	1849-2344	816 -1067
1908	2345-2602	1068- 1183
1909	2603- 3070	1184 - 1395
1910	3071- 3547	1396 - 1615
1911	3548- 3964	1616 - 1791
1912	3965- 4496	1792 - 1998
1913	4497-5126	1999-2246

Year	Volume #	Nat'l Archives Reel #
1914	5127-5505	2247-2391
1915	5506-5561	2392-2446
1916	5662 -5836	2447 -2508
1917	5837 -5986	2509 -2558
1920	6333 - 6665	2715 -2902
1921	6666 -6990	2903-3067
1922	6991 -7399	3068 - 3237
1923	7400 -7856	3238 -3435
1924	7857 - 8219	3436 -3590
1925	8220-8588	3591 -3778
1926	8589 -8964	3779 -3987
1927	8965 -9344	3988 -4191
1928	9345 -9739	4192 -4406
1929	9740 -10142	4407 -4653
1930	10143 - 10588	4654 -4892
1931	1058 - 11000	4893 -5090
1932	11001 - 11371	5091 - 5276

Copies of U.S. Passenger Lists

The major port of Jewish immigration was New York. During the great Eastern European exodus around the turn of the last century, immigrants originally landed at Castle (Kessel) Garden at the tip of Manhattan. That center quickly became too small to handle the numbers of immigrants and the Federal government converted Ellis Island into the new immigration reception area by 1902.

Other important ports of arrival for Jews were Philadelphia, Boston, Baltimore, and Galveston.

Records of the small ports on the Canadian border were found recently. These records are referred to as the *St. Albans Lists Vermont District Records.* Immigrants were quickly processed by U.S. Immigration and placed on trains to their final destination.

There are two types of indexes, Soundex and Alphabetical. Use the chart to find what records are available for your ancestors port.

Guide to Popular Jewish Ports of Entry Records

Port	Microfilm Series	Index	Microfilm Series	List
Baltimore	T 520	1897-1952	T 844	1891-1909
Boston	T 790 T 521	1899-1940 1902-1906 a	T 843	1891-1943
Galveston	M 1357	1896-1906 a	M 1358	1896-1958
New York	T 519 T 621 T 612 M 1417	1897-1902 1902-1943 1906-1942 a 1944-1948	T 715	18971957
Philadelphia	T 526 T 791	1883-1948 1906-1926 a	T 840	1906-1926
St. Albans District	M 1461 M 1462 M 1463	1895-1924 1895-1924 a 1924-1952	M 1464 M 1465	1895-1924 1924-1949

If you do not live near a National Archives branch library, you may order copies through the Reference Services Branch of the National Archives. Write to:

NWCTB
700 Pennsylvania Av NW
Washington DC 20408

They will search for your ancestor's record for $ 10 if the list is indexed. This fee is payable **only** when the requested records are found. Use *NATF Form 81 "Order for copies of Passenger Arrival Records."* Provide:

- □ Port of Arrival,
- □ Approximate Date of Arrival
- □ Age of Passenger
- □ Accompanying persons

If you have used the *Index to Passenger Arrival*, include all information from the index as well. Passenger Arrival Records can be ordered through your local Family History Center microfilm loan system.

You can go on-line to search for the actual reel numbers
www.nara.gov/publications/microfilm/immigrant/immpass.html
Forms: inquire@nara.gov

Passenger Arrival Worksheet

Passenger's Name	Soundex Code	Index Reel #	Vol. #	Pg. #	Line #	Record Reel #	√	Ports

Photographs of Passenger Arrival Ships

A photographic copy is available for most steamships of the nineteenth and twentieth centuries. You may write to the following for price and availability of photographs.

Steamship Historical Society
414 Pelton Avenue
Staten Island, NY 10310

University of Baltimore Library
1420 Maryland Avenue
Baltimore, Md. 21201

Mariners Museum
Newport News, Va. 23606

Sample Letter

Dear Sir or Madam,

I am interested in obtaining a photograph and information about the ship the **S.S. Vadeerland** that sailed from **Antwerp** around 1907. Please notify me of costs of the same.

Sincerely,

Your Name

Passports

Some immigrants returned to the old country for a visit or to bring other members of the family back to America. The new citizen did not want to chance being retained or conscripted into the military of their former country. A passport was proof of American citizenship. It was only after World War I that passports were required of all American citizens traveling abroad. The National Archives has American passport applications from 1791 to 1925.

The passport application for a person who was naturalized prior to 1906 included their naturalization records as proof of citizenship. Between 1906 and 1925, you can expect to find in the passport application:

☐ Name of the applicant
☐ Residence, Occupation
☐ Date and Place of birth

☐ Name, Place of birth of spouse and/or children
☐ Date of naturalization
☐ Court of naturalization
☐ Name of the ship
☐ Date and Port of arrival in U.S.

Records over seventy-five (75) years can be obtained by writing to the:

National Archives and Records Center
National Records Center Building
4205 Suitland Rd.
Suitland, MD 20409

Include with your request:

☐ Name of the applicant
☐ Place and approximate date of application

Records less than seventy-five years, must include proof of death.

Military Records

 Military records are another source of information about your immigrant relative.

A Register of Enlistments in the U.S. Army exists. Many immigrants became citizens by enlisting in the Army, especially during the Civil and Spanish-American Wars. These records are available through the National Archives M233: *Registers of Enlistments in the U.S. Army, 1789-1914.* The records are arranged first chronologically and then alphabetically.

General Index to Pension Files 1861-1934 Microfilm series T 288

If you know the unit your ancestor served in you can search the *Organizational Index to Pension Files of Veterans Who Served Between 1861 and 1900.* This is a fully indexed and includes Civil War, Spanish-American, Indian wars and World War I applications. The veterans generally served in the U.S. Army between 1861 and 1917. The index is arranged alphabetically by state, then regiment, then veterans' surname.

Organizational Index to Pension Files 1861-1900
Microfilm SeriesT 289

WWI Veterans Information

Records of WWI veterans can include many items of genealogical information. Included can be:

- marriage
- citizenship
- next of kin
- medical

If you are a relative of the individual you may obtain a copy of his service record by writing to:

National Personnel Records Center
Attn.: Army Records
9700 Page Blvd.
St. Louis, MO 63132

Provide as much info as possible including

- Full Name
- Service Number
- Social Security Number
- Period of Service
- State from which entered service
- Branch of Service
- Date of Birth
- Place of Birth
- Proof of death or signature of serviceman

Homestead Records

The Homestead Act of May 20, 1862, allowed settlers to acquire free land as long as they lived on the land and improved it. The requirement also included the fact that the Homesteader had to be a citizen. Many immigrants filed their Declaration of Intention to qualify.

You must know the legal description of the land to research the information. You can then write to:

Bureau of Land Management
Eastern States Office
350 S Pickett St.
Alexandria, VA 22304

For Wyoming, Kansas and Nebraska write to:

Bureau of Land Management
PO Box 1828
Cheyenne, WY 82001.

Once you have the patent case file number, you can write for the Homestead papers.

National Archives
Reference Branch
General Archives Division
Washington, D.C. 20408

The application dates are 1863-1908. In the file is the application, the names of two witnesses, and the final certificates of homestead patent. The file may contain references to naturalization.

*H*olocaust

Yiskor

and

Memorial Books

JEWS IN BIALYSTOK AFTER THE W.

PINKAS PRUZ'ANY AND ITS VICINITY

(Bereze, Malch, Shershev, Seltz and Lineve)

Chronicle of six Communities perished in the Holocaust

Holocaust Research

More than six million Jews were murdered during the Shoah (Holocaust). Almost **every Jew lost a relative**. Many people are unaware of the names and relationships between themselves and these peoples.

Speculate that your great-grandparents did not accompany their children to America in 1902. Probably one of there relatives stayed in Europe to care for them. That child married and had children.

Over the decades connection to the relatives in America was lost. It is now possible to determine if these relatives lived or perished in the single largest disaster in modern times to befall the Jewish people.

Many people believe that all the records of Jewish existence in Europe were lost, yet the Shoah is the most documented event of the twentieth century. Records are available for research from many sources.

Yiskor and Memorial Books

A Memorial Book traces the history of a Jewish community. There are more than 800 Yiskor books written. The book usually has a narrative section on the town's history, a map of the town, photographs of many of its citizens with commentaries, a list of known victims and survivors. Sometimes victims from various *pogroms*, are listed as well.

The books are written primarily in Yiddish and Hebrew, but depending on the authors, you may find some with English and/or Spanish sections. Many of these books were published by the *Landsmanshaften*. A list of these may be obtained through YIVO. These books can also be requested through Interlibrary Loan from the Price Library.

Most Yizkor books were published in the 1950's and 1960's in very limited quantities. They are not only difficult to find, but also quite expensive to purchase. Currently these books sell between $ 80 to $ 500. There is a project underway to locate and translate all these books.

Check your local Holocaust Center to see which Yizkor books are available. Some of the major collections are located at Yad Vashem (Jerusalem), the Library of Congress (Washington) "http://www.loc.gov." You will also find them at:

- YIVO
- New York Public Library
- Jewish Theological Seminary
- Yeshiva University (New York)
- UCLA (Los Angeles)
- Holocaust Center-North California (San Francisco)
- Harvard and Brandeis University
- Price Judaic Library (Gainesville, FL)
- Jewish Public Library of Montreal.

For more information see the information file available on the World Wide Web
http://www.jewishgen.org/infofiles/yizret.txt
    or by e-mail   yizret@jewishgen.org

Yad Vashem

Yad Vashem is the main repository of information about the Shoah. This library contains 100,000+ volumes that include 800+ Yiskor books. On file are more than three million *Pages of Testimony.* Relatives, neighbors and friends of the victims contributed the information. Each *Page of Testimony* contains the name of the victim, their parents, spouse, and any children. Included are the places of residence during the war, and circumstances of death. The birth and death dates and the places of each event are included. The name, address and relationship of person submitting are also given. If lucky, you can then trace this person.

Yad Vashem- Resource Center
P.O. Box 3477
Jerusalem, Israel 91034
02-972-2-751611
Fax: 02-972-2-433511
www.yvs.shani.net

The following pages contain the locations of some of the research facilities available.

U.S. Holocaust Memorial Research Center
100 Raoul Wallenberg Place
5th Floor
Washington, D.C. 20024-2150
(202) 488-2690
Fax: (202) 488-2690

Registry of Jewish Holocaust Survivors
(formerly American Gathering of Jewish Holocaust Survivors)

Archive and Research Library. Extensive Memorial Book/Yiskor book collection. Photograph collection. Check town, then the surname. A list of more than 85,000 survivors in the U.S. and Canada, maintained by the U.S. Holocaust Research Center in Washington.
http://www.ushmm.org

There is a searchable database of the Auschwitz prisoner registration forms, May 1942 through October 1944. **www.ushmm.org/via-bin/via_form/registry**

Gedenkbukh

This two-volume book   contains the names of approximately 128,000 German Jews who died in the Shoah. This book is available at most larger research libraries and almost all Judaic libraries. The information included is the birth date and place of the victim and the place they were deported to. For more information see Information file available:

www.jewishgen.org/infofiles/gedenk.txt
or by e-mail gedenk@jewishgen.org

The International Tracing Service

American Red Cross
Holocaust & War Victims
 Tracing Information Center
4700 Mount Hope Drive
Baltimore, MD 21215
          (301) 764-5311
Fax: (410) 764-4638

This nonprofit organization helps individuals locate family members that disappeared during the years 1933 through 1952. The emphasis is on World War II victims interned in concentration, forced labor or death camps. The Center works closely with the International Committee of the Red Cross. They have more than forty-six million documents relating to the fourteen million victims. They also will help relatives separated and believed to be living in the United States or other countries. Expect to wait at least a year for results.

International Tracing Service
Grosse Allee 5-9
34454 Arolsen, Germany

It is preferable to contact your local chapter of the American Red Cross versus Germany.

The U.S. National Archives Military Archives Division

Has microfilms of many captured German records from World War II, including concentration camp records.

Babi Yar Memorial Fund

7, Nemanskaya Street
252103 Kiev 103
Ukraine
Telephone: 2959604   296-3961
Fax: 2958044   228-7272

Illya Vevitas and Klara Vinocur are the Directors of this organization. If you believe your relative may have perished in the slaughter of Babi Yar, contact them for further information.

Hidden Child Foundation - ADL

823 United Nations Plaza
New York, NY 10017
          (212) 490-2525
Fax: (212) 867-0779

This organization specializes in the network of "hidden children" and their stories of survival.

Dallas Center for Holocaust Studies

7900 Northhaven Road
Dallas, TX 75230
          (214) 750-4672
Fax: (214) 368-4709

This is one of the larger centers and has a library consisting of more than 2500 volumes of material relating to the Shoah.

World Federation of Bergen-Belsen Associations

P.O. Box 232
Lenox Hill Station
New York, NY 10021
          (212) 752-3387

Holocaust Center of Northern California
639 14th Avenue
San Francisco, CA 94118
(415) 751-6040, 751-6041
Fax: (415) 751-6735
This library has more than 8000 volumes of material on the Shoah. It also has translated the Yizkor books for Kosow Lacki, Poland and Kobrin, Poland

Holocaust Center of UJF-Greater Pittsburgh
242 Mc Kee Place
Pittsburgh, PA 15213
(412) 682-7111   Fax (412) 681-3980

The library has more than 2,500 volumes

Holocaust Learning Center
David Posnack Jewish Center
5850 South Pine Island Road
Davie, FL 33328
(954) 434-0499 ext. 314
Fax: (954) 434-1741

The library contains more than 1,000 volumes

Holocaust Memorial Resource and
Education Center of Central Florida
851 N. Maitland Avenue
Maitland, FL 32751
(407) 628-0555
Fax: (407) 628-0555

Has unpublished memoirs, Memorial books and Survivor registers. 2,500 volume library.

Holocaust Resource Center & Archives
Queensborough Community. College
222-05 56th Avenue
Bayside, NY 11364
(718) 225-1617
Fax: (718) 423-9620

5,000 volume Library

Holocaust Oral History Archive
Gratz College
Tuttleman Library
Old York Road & Melrose Ave
Melrose Park, PA 19126
      (215) 635-7300 X. 30
Fax: (215) 635-7320

Memorial books and Survivor Registers.

Holocaust Resource Center
Kean College -Thompson Library
Second Floor
Kean College
Union, NJ 07083
      (908) 527-3049

2,500 Volume Library

Leo Baeck Institute
129 E. 73 St. (Moving late 1998)
New York, NY 10021
      (212) 744-6400
Fax: (212) 988-1305
Extensive library. German/Austrian

Rockland Center for Holocaust Studies, Inc.
17 S. Madison Ave
Spring Valley, NY 10977
(914) 356-2700

Library has 1,500 volumes

Simon Wiesenthal Research Center
9760 W. Pico Blvd.
Los Angeles, CA 90035
      (310) 553-9036
Fax: (310) 533-8007

Extensive library with 20,000 volumes and extensive Yiskor/Memorial book collection. Survivor Registers.

Search Bureau for Missing Relatives
> P.O. Box 92
> Jerusalem 91000
> Israel.
> 02-612471, 02-612472

Dynamo Batya Unterschatz can help find anyone that has emigrated to Israel.

Bet Hatefutsot (Museum of the Diaspora)

> **DOROT Genealogy Center**
> P.O. Box 39359
> Tel Aviv 61392 ISRAEL.
> Telephone (03)6462062

Diana Sommers, director has amassed 200,000 individuals its database. The database can be accessed only in person or by writing. The Dorot Center will accept family trees on a diskette in GEDCOM format only.

HIAS (Hebrew Immigrant Aid Society)

HIAS (Hebrew Immigrant Aid Society) is the combination of the United Service for New Americans (USNA) and the immigration services of the American Joint Distribution Committee (AJDC). Most immigrants were greeted either Castle Garden or Ellis Island in New York, the ports of Boston, Philadelphia, etc. by members of HIAS from about 1892 on. The members of HIAS helped the immigrant through the landing process by acting as translators and generally watched over them. Records are available for those landings after 1908.

HIAS assisted more than 70,000 Holocaust families in the 1940's and 1950's. They maintain case files on these persons, and will search for a $25 fee.

> HIAS World Headquarters
> 200 Park Avenue South
> New York, NY 10003
> (212) 674-6800

Record Search Request

Please fill out a separate form for each inquiry requested. Please note we have records beginning in 1908.

Family Name (Last name) _____
(include spelling variations)

First Name _____

Names of Others Traveling Together with above:

_____

Date of Birth _____

Country of Birth _____

City of Birth _____

Date of Arrival _____ Port of Entry _____

Your Name _____

Your Address _____

_____

Relationship to "Head of Household":

_____

> NOTE: Records generally are for the "head of household," therefore, it is best to focus your request on the head of household which will then provide names of accompanying family members.

Jewish Genealogical People Finder (JGPF)

> The JGPF is a database of family trees on microfiche. The 310,000 individuals, whose entries were submitted by Jewish genealogists contain the following information: date and place of birth, date and place of death, parents' names and spouses' name. Family trees in GEDCOM format may be submitted without charge. Send diskettes to:

> Avotaynu, Inc.
> PO Box 900
> Teaneck, NJ 07666
> **www.avotaynu.com**

The Jewish Genealogical Family Finder(JGFF)

This paper copy database contains a surname and town names index. You may locate other persons researching the same names and towns. Available on **jewishgen.org** or at any JGS meeting.

Institutions with Significant Yizkor Book Collections

Los Angeles
> **Hebrew Union College**
> **Frances Henry Library**
> 3077 University Avenue
> Los Angeles, CA 90007
>
> **UCLA - University Research Library**
> 405 Hilgard Avenue
> Los Angeles, CA 90024
>
> **University of Judaism**
> **Jack M. & Bell Ostrow Library**
> 15600 Mulholland Drive
> Los Angeles, CA 90077

Florida
> **University of Florida**
> **Price Library of Judaica**
> Rm. 18, Library East
> Gainesville, FL 32611
> > (available on Interlibrary Loan)
>
> **Florida Atlantic University**
> **Wimberly Library-Freiberg Collection**
> 777 Glades Rd
> Boca Raton, FL 33431
>
> **Holocaust Documentation & Education Center**
> F I U-N. Miami Campus
> 3000 N.E. 145 St
> North Miami, FL 33181

Illinois

Hebrew Theological College Library
7135 Carpenter Road
Skokie, IL 60076

Spertus College-Asher Library
618 South Michigan Avenue
Chicago, IL 60605

Maryland

Baltimore Hebrew University
Joseph Meyerhoff Library
5800 Park Heights Avenue
Baltimore, MD 21215

Massachusetts

Brandeis University - Goldfarb Library
Waltham, MA 02254

Harvard University -Widener Library, Judaica Dept.
Room M
Cambridge, MA 02138

Hebrew Union College
Jacob & Rose Grossman Library
43 Hawes St.
Brookline, MA 02146

Michigan

Holocaust Memorial Center
6602 W. Maple Road
W. Bloomfield, MI 48322

Missouri

Washington University-Olin Library
Forsyth & Skinker Blvd.
St. Louis, MO 63105

New York

Bund Archives-Jewish Labor Movement
25 E. 21 St. 3rd Fl

New York, NY 10010

Center for Holocaust Studies
1609 Avenue J
Brooklyn, NY 11230

Jewish Theological Seminary
3080 Broadway
New York, NY 10027

New York Public Library
Jewish Division
42nd St. & Fifth Avenue
New York, NY 10018

YIVO Library
1048 Fifth Avenue (moving 1999)
New York, NY 10028

Yeshiva University
Mendel Gottesman Library
500 W. 185 St.
New York, NY 10033

Ohio

Hebrew Union College-Jewish Institute of Religion
Klau Library
3101 Clifton Avenue
Cincinnati, OH 45220

Pennsylvania
Gratz College
10th St. & Tabor Rd.
Philadelphia, PA 19141

Tennessee
Jewish Federation of Nashville
801 Perry Warner Blvd.
Nashville, TN 37205

Texas
University of Texas
Perry Castandeda Library

PO Box P, University Station
Austin, TX 78713

Washington, D.C.
Library of Congress-African & Middle Eastern Division
Adams Bldg.--Hebraic Section
110 Second St. SE
Washington, D.C. 20540

Canada
Jewish Public Library
5151 Chemin de la Cote Ste-Catherine
Montreal, H3W 1M6 Quebec

Albert J. Latner
Jewish Public Library
4600 Bathurst St.
Willowdale, M2R 3V2 Ontario

John T. Robarts Research Library
University of Toronto
130 St. George St.
Toronto, M5S 1A1 Ontario

Organizing

your

Data

Organizing Your Material

You have collected an enormous amount of data at this point. It is time to pause, evaluate the material, and **Organize**. Start with the following:

① Four, (4) three-inch loose leaf binders. One for each family line, (maternal grandmother, maternal grandfather, paternal grandmother, paternal grandfather).

② Index dividers for each binder. Have a section for each child of your grandparents. Eventually you may have to get binders for each child.

③ Plastic sheet protectors. These sheet are available at office supply stores and will protect your material from constant handling.

④ Archival quality sheet protectors. These protect the collected documents from damage.

⑤ A **Family Chart** for each relative.

⑥ An **Ahnetafel Chart** for the beginning of each binder.

⑦ A **Pedigree Chart** for each section.

⑧ A **Descendant's Chart** for each progenitor.

How do you record the information about your cousins and their children? This is done through the **Descendant's Chart**. This includes cousins, aunts and uncles, nieces and nephews. Use the chart below as a guide for making your own descendants form. In the chart below, the first progenitor is the Great-Great Grandfather.

Family Chart For _____	

Hebrew Name: _____

          Paternal ☐
Named for Maternal ☐ _____

Birth Date: _____

City: _____ County: _____ State: _____

Marriage Date: _____

City: _____ County: _____ State: _____

Your Father's Name: _____

Hebrew Name: _____

          Paternal ☐
Named for Maternal ☐ _____

Birth Date: _____

City: _____ County: _____ State: _____

Date of Death: _____

City: _____ County: _____ State: _____

Place of Burial: _____

City: _____ County: _____ State: _____

Date of Marriage: _____

City: _____ County: _____ State: _____

Other Marriages: _____

Your Mother's Name (Name at Birth): _____

Hebrew Name: _____

          Paternal ☐
Named for Maternal ☐ _____

Birth Date: _____

City: _____ County: _____ State: _____

Date of Death: _____

City: _____ County: _____ State: _____

Place of Burial: _____

City: _____ County: _____ State: _____

Other Marriages: _____

Your Spouse (Name at Birth): _____

Hebrew Name: _____

Paternal ☐
Named for Maternal ☐ _____

Birth Date: _____

City: _____ County: _____ State: _____

Date of Death: _____

City: _____ County: _____ State: _____

Place of Burial: _____

City: _____ County: _____ State: _____

Other Marriages: _____

Children of _____(mother)

& _____ (father)

	NAME	BORN	TOWN/ COUNTY	STATE/ COUNTY	SPOUSE
1					
2					
3					

Current Addresses

1._____

_____

2. _____

_____

3._____

_____

Ahnetafel Chart

Fill in the *AHNETAFEL CHART* below. An Ahnetafel chart records your direct ancestors in text format.

Generation 1 : _____
You

Generation 2 : _____
Your Father

_____
Your Mother

Generation 3 : _____
Paternal Grandfather

_____
Paternal Grandmother

_____
Maternal Grandfather

_____
Maternal Grandmother

Generation 4: _____
Paternal Great-Grandfather

_____
Paternal Great-Grandmother

_____
Paternal Great-Grandfather

_____
Paternal Great-Grandmother

_____
Maternal Great- Grandfather

_____
Maternal Great-Grandmother

_____
Maternal Great- Grandfather

_____
Maternal Great-Grandmother

Pedigree Chart

Descendant's Chart

Great-grandfather .... 0_____

Great-Grandmother .... _____

Grandfather .... 1_____

Grandmother .... _____

Aunt\Uncle .... 2_____

Spouse .... _____

Cousin .... 3 _____

Second Cousin. .... 4_____

Cousin .... 3 _____

Aunt or Uncle .... 2_____

Spouse .... _____

Cousin .... 3_____

Cousin .... 3 _____

Your Mother/Father .... 2_____

Spouse of parent .... _____

Brother/Sister .... 3_____

Nieces/Nephew .... 4_____

Brother .... 3_____

Nieces/Nephew .... 4 _____

YOU .... 3_____

Your Child .... 4_____

Your Grandchildren .... 5_____

Gr. Grandchildren ... . 6_____

Your Child .... 4_____

Your Grandchildren .... 5_____

Gr. Grandchildren .... 6 _____

Computers

Computers enable you to organize data efficiently and update this information without having to retype or re glue your charts. After visiting your relatives, you discover that Aunt Esther was born on February 10, 1867 not March 6, 1859. This means that you have to change her family chart, descendant chart, and any place her name appears.

Consider what would happen if you've made up all your charts and then discovered Aunt Esther was not the oldest child of Grandpa Isaac, but the third born child. You would then have to once again redo all your charts. With a computer, all you need to do is change the information on Aunt Esther's file card. The computer automatically changes **every** document. You can then just print out a new copy.

You receive a letter in the mail from a person who might be related to you. Rather than run down to the copy store and photocopy all your records, you can search your records, see if there is possibly a match and mail your information out within a minute. You can even exchange information on a disk. You can add the new information to any of your programs. When you have hundreds of names, this becomes important.

Printing out charts is another advantage. These charts can list birthdays. They can also list all persons with the same first initial with the same grandparent. The computer can sort your information and provide you with a list of all relatives living in a city you are about to visit.

If you do not personally own a computer, check with friends, and relatives to see if you can use theirs while you evaluate your needs. Even easier, use the computer at your local Family History Center or local library to enter data entry. At the FHC they even provide a genealogy program to make entry easy.

More genealogy software is available in IBM Windows format and is generally less expensive. Decide which software types (IBM or MAC) you plan on using before buying the computer. Check to see what type your friends or relatives use. Learning to use a computer is easier with a friendly person by your side.

Consider the ease of using a program and the costs. The average program retails about $19 to $100. Almost all programs are *Gedcom* and offer assistance.

I cannot stress enough the importance of using a Gedcom compatible genealogy program. GedCom is the acronym for Genealogical Exchange of Data. Gedcom allows you to shift information between different genealogy programs. This is essential. Anyone that is computer literate can make a flow chart. But will you be able to import the information of cousin Yossi's 200 relatives without retyping everything? Many databases enable you to download family charts and files, but often they are in Gedcom format.

Consider your needs as a Jewish researcher. Some programs do not allow for the setting up of custom "fields". Fields allow you to enter data that you want to track. I use a custom field for Hebrew names. I do not want a field for christening to appear on my printouts. This can be important. Other fields you might use are: whom someone is named after, Yarzheit dates, immigration dates, etc.

There are too many programs on the market today to give a review of all of them. Look for a program that is

    □ easy to use
    □ will allow unlimited entries of names?
    □ will allow you to changing the data entry fields?
    □ Gedcom

If at a later date you want to change your program, you can Gedcom the data out. Most programs today work with your word processing program. This can be important when you want to have an extended story. Check to make sure the program you are considering allows this.

We all love charts. Does your program allow for editing or the charts-squeezing of generations? This can become important when your charts number 15-60 pages.

The World Wide Web

We are now living in the information age. The world wide web has been nicknamed the information highway, and indeed it is. You can now do "*on-line*" research. Only a year ago, you couldn't do any research on-line except maybe check out telephone numbers. Today, there are hundreds of search pages where you can actually do research. It would be impossible to give all the "*addresses*" to do this research, but there are a few that will lead you to others. My three favorites are JewishGen, Ancestry, and the JGS of Great Britain.

JewishGen-http://www.jewishgen.org

The most important web address for Jewish researchers is JewishGen. This site was started just a few years ago by Susan King. It has grown and now has searchable databases. Some of the searchable databases include:

- JewishGen Family Finder
- Shtetl Seeker
  find your ancestral town even if you don't know the correct spelling
- Vsia Rossia 1895
  Census records from Ukrainian Regions
- Jewish Religious Personnel in Russia 1853-54

- Phoenix Project
    12,000 people from the Brest Ghetto
- Grodno Gubernia 1912 Voters List
- Jewish Record Indexing of Poland
    200,000 Birth, Marriage, Death
- LDS Microfilm Master List of Poland
- HaMagid Lithuanian Donors 1871-72
- HaMelitz Lithuanian Donors
- Jewish Families in Northern Germany
- Bristol, England Cemetery Database
- Jews of London (pre 1850)
- Obituary Databases-1990's to present
    Boston, Cleveland, Chicago
- Jewish-American Civil War Database
    both Union and Confederate
    Provides name, rank and regiment number so
    that you can then send for the Pension records.
- American Jewish Yearbook 1948-1994
- Links to Special Interest Groups (SIGS)
- Links to JGS organizations with Web pages

JGS-Great Britain Home Page
  http://ort.org/jgsgb/info1.htm
  Incredible home page that links you to every other
  database of Jewish interest.

Ancestry
  http://www.ancestry.com
  Free and fee databases. Now includes databases of
  Jewish interest. One of largest sites.
  Free sites:
- Social Security Death Index
  www.ancestry.com/ssdi/advanced.html
- World War I Civil Draft Registrations
  Fee based sites:
- Biographical Dictionary of Canadian Jews
    1897-1914
- Wurttemberg Emigration Index
- Various state records

New York Public Library
http://nypl.org/research/chss/lhg/research.html
> Great search engine for holdings and genealogical information available for New York. Includes lists of Index's for Vital Records.

Unites States Holocaust Memorial Archives
http://www.ushmm.org
> The archives of the Holocaust Museum in Washington have a wealth of information.

The Poor Jews' Temporary Shelter Database
http://www.its.uct.ac.za/shelter.htm
> List the names, previous city and destinations of persons awaiting ships to complete their journey. Especially helpful for persons whose ancestors used indirect routes to their final destination. This list will tell you if your relatives went to U.S. Australia, South America etc.

> Federation of East European Family History Societies
> http:/feefhs.org
> http:/feefhs.org/maps/indexmap.html
> Links to maps and East European databases

Dormant Swiss Bank Accounts
http://www.dormantaccounts.ch/jul/_list.html
> You might find monies due you and the names of your relatives in the infamous Swiss Bank Accounts. Searchable by name.

National Archives
http://www.nara.gov /genealogy/genindex.html
> Organize what you will be researching by checking reel numbers before going to the Archives. On line catalogues include:

> □ 1790-1890 Federal Population Census
> □ 1900 Federal Population Census
> □ 1910 Federal Population Census
> □ 1920 Federal Population Census

      □ Federal Court Records
      □ Immigrant and Passenger Arrivals
      □ Genealogical & Biographical Research

Federation of East European Family History Societies
      http:/feefhs.org
      http:/feefhs.org/maps/indexmap.html
      Links to maps and East European databases

Genealogy Home Page
      http://www.genhomepage.com/jewish.html
      □ Frequently Asked Questions
      □ Links to Sephardim organizations
      □ Calendar conversions-Gregorian, Julian, Hebrew
      □ Jamaican Jewish Historical Society Link

Hebrew National Orphan Homes
      www.scruz.net/~elias/hnoh/usjorph6a.html
      Searchable databases if your ancestor was placed in an orphanage or foster home. Examples are:
      □ Hebrew Orphan Asylum-1,055 children from the 1920 Census
      □ Brooklyn Hebrew Orphan Asylum-1925 State
      □ Census information
      □ Listing of Jewish Orphanages
      □ Lists of names and locations

http://www.yahoo.com/arts/humanities/history/genealogy
      Connects to many other sites.

Every day a new database is found. New records are coming from Germany, the former Soviet Union and other countries. The Mormons have a 102-year privacy restriction while the Federal government 72 years. In the year 2002, the 1930 census will be available. Be ready. Start now.

Your unique heritage is your gift to the succeeding generations. Take the time to record it for your children, your children's children and for all those that follow.

Where to Write

for What

The next pages contain the names and addresses of where to write for information.

Judaica Libraries

Library	Address	Holdings
Agudath Israel of America Orthodox Jewish Archives	84 William Street New York, NY 10038 (212) 797-9000	Orthodox Yeshiva students 1910+ Divorces from Northeast Rabbinical courts 1910-1948 Lists of students and Jewish schools in Poland and Lithuania 1937-1939
American Jewish Joint Distribution Committee (ADC)	711 Third Ave New York, NY 10017 (212) 687-6200	Records of relief funds sent by family members to Europe 1914-1918. Refugee files.
American Jewish Historical Society	2 Thornton Road Waltham, MA 02154 (617) 891-8110 (617) 899-9208 Fax	Oldest ethnic historical organization
American Jewish Archives Hebrew Union College	3101 Clifton Ave Cincinnati, Oh 45220-2404 (513)221-1875 FAX: (513) 221-7812	Collection of family histories. Reform congregational records
Bund Archives	Afran Center 25 E. 21 St New York, NY 10010 (212) 473-5101	Newspapers from 1897-1920, Mailing lists, Czarist Russia Workmen's Circle records
Center for Jewish History	New York, N.Y. opening 1999	See YIVO; Leo Beck
Hebrew Union College	see American Jewish Archives	

Library	Address	Holdings
Hebrew Union College Klau Library Department of Religion Concordia University	1 W. 4 St New York, NY 10012 (212) 674-5300	Cemetery records Europe and US. Portuguese Inquisition Records (1541-1820) Histories of European Communities American Jewish Year Book 1899+ Assoc. for the Protection of Jewish Immigrants Philadelphia 1884-1921
Hebrew Union College Library	3077 University Ave Los Angeles, Ca 00007 3796 (213) 749-3426	
National Museum of American Jewish History	55 North 5th Street Philadelphia, PA 19106 (215) 923-3811I	
HIAS (Hebrew Immigrant Aid Society)	333 7th Avenue New York, NY 10005 (212) 967-4100	Immigrants helped by HIAS Index cards 1909-1979 1980+ computerized Joint Distribution Committee Index
Jewish Theological Seminary Archives	3080 Broadway New York, NY 10027 (212) 744-6400; 678-8000	Rabbinical and Congregational Records
Leo Baeck Institute Library	129 E. 73 St New York, NY 10021	German-Jewish Records German/Austrian Empire community record Circumcision and Vital Records for Germany/Austrian Empire

Library	Address	Holdings
Library of Congress Geography	1 & Independence Av Washington, DC 20024 (202) 707-5127	
Library of Congress Reference	(202) 707-6500; 6345, 5535, 5510	
Library of Congress Hebraic Section	Adams Bldg- 110 Second St. SE Washington, DC 20540	Yiskor books
New York Public Library	42nd St & Fifth Ave New York, NY 10016 (212) 930-0830 Newspapers	Judaic Rm: Community histories Yiskor books Map Rm
New York University Wagner Labor Archives	70 Washington Sq. S New York, NY 10012 (212) 998-2630	Labor Movement Collection Records of NY Public Employees Entertainment, United Auto Workers
National Museum of American Jewish History	55 North 5th Street Philadelphia, PA 19106 (215) 923-3811	
Philadelphia Jewish Archives Balch Institute	18 S. 7 St Philadelphia, PA 19106 (215) 925-8090	HIAS Collection, Landsmanshaftn records Philadelphia area synagogues Orphans' records 1855-1974
Southwest Jewish Archives	1052 North Highland Avenue Tuscon, AZ 85721 (520) 621-5774	http://dizzy.library.arizona.edu/images/swja/info.html

Library	Address	Holdings
Yeshiva University Archives	2520 Amsterdam Ave Rm. 405 & 5th FL New York, NY 10033 (212) 960-5451	Central Relief Committee (1914-1959) Jewish Communities in German (1605-1965) Natl Council of Women Immigrant Collection Synagogue Records (1917-1967) Hebrew Periodicals
YIVO	555 W. 57 St 11th Floor New York, NY 10019 (212) 224-6080 fax: (212) 292-1892 moving 1000 **www.baruch.cuny.edu/ yivo**	Landsmanshaftn Archive HIAS Ellis Island (1905-1923) Photograph Collection Genealogy Collection

National Archive Research Centers

Washington, D.C.

Central Info Division
National Archives
Washington, D.C. 20408
(202) 523-3220

* National Records Center
Washington, D.C. 20409
(202) 763-7000

National Archives
8601 Adelphi Road
College Park, MD 20740-6001
(301) 713-6800;
Fax (301) 713-6905
E-mail:
inquire @ arch2.nara.gov
Gopher.nara.gov
  http:/www.nara.gov

Alaska

654 W. Third Avenue
Anchorage, AK 99501-2145
(907) 271-2441 Fax: 271-2442

Atlanta-Southeast

National Archives
1557 St. Joseph Avenue
East Point, Ga 30344-2593
(404) 763-7477 Fax: 763-7033
AL, GA,. FL, KY, MI, NC, SC

Boston - New England

National Archives
380 Trapelo Road
Waltham, MA 02154-6399
(781) 647-8104; Fax: 647-8088
CT, ME, MA, NH, RI, VT

Chicago - Great Lakes

National Archives
7358 S. Pulaski Road
Chicago, IL 60629-5898
(312) 581-7816; Fax: 886-7883
IL, ID, MI, MN, OH, WI.

Denver-Rocky Mountain

Bld. 48,
Denver Federal Center
PO Box 25307
Denver, CO 80225-0307
(303) 236-0817 Fax: 236-9297
CO, MT, ND, SD, UT, WY

Fort Worth

National Archives
PO Box 6216
501 W. Felix Street-Bldg.1
Fort Worth, TX 76115-0216
(817 334-5515   Fax: 334-5511
AK, LA, NM, OK, TX

Los Angeles - Pacific SW

National Archives
PO Box 6719
 24000 Avila Road
 E. Entrance
Laguna Niguel, CA 92677
(714) 643-4220 Fax: 360-2624
AZ, So Cal, NV (Clark Cty)

New York - Northeast

National Archives
201 Varick Street
New York, NY 10014-4811
(212) 337-1300; Fax: 337-1306
NJ, NY, PR, VI

Philadelphia - Mid Atlantic

National Archives
900 Market Streets; Rm. 1350
Philadelphia, PA 19107-4292
(215) 597-3000; Fax: 597-2303
DE, PA, MD,VA., WV

St. Louis - Central Plains

Federal Record Center
2312 E. Bannister Road
Kansas City, MO 64131-3011
(816) 926-6920 ; Fax: 926-6982
IW, KS., MO, NE

Pittsfield - Northeast

10 Conte Dr
Pittsfield, MA 01201-8230
(413) 445-6885; Fax 445-7305
Military Service, Pension, Bounty
Land Warrants

San Francisco - Pacific Sierra

National Archives
1000 Commodore Drive
San Bruno, CA 94066-
(650) 876-9001; Fax: 876-0920
No. Cal., HW, NV

Seattle - Pacific Northwest

National Archives
6125 Sand Point Way NE
Seattle, WA 981157-999
(206) 526-6501; Fax: 526-6575
ID, OR, Washington State

St. Louis

National Personnel Records
9700 Page Blvd.
St. Louis, MO 63132
(314) 538-4175; Fax: 876-0920
Post 1930's Census

Available on line at: http://www.nara.gov.regional/nrmenu.html

Where to Write for Vital Records

B= Birth,   D= Death,   M= Marriage,   DV= Divorce

C A	Dept. of Health Svc. Vital Statistics Sect. PO Box 730241 Sacramento, CA 94244-0241	(916) 445-2684 fax: (800) 858-5553	B, D, M 1905+ Dv- 1962+ Earlier records maintained by County Recorder M, Dv- County
F L	Office of Vital Statistics PO Box 210 1217 Pearl Street Jacksonville, FL 32231	(904) 359-6900	B-Apr 1865 + D-Majority 1917+ M, Dv June 6, 1927+
G A	Dept of Human Resources Vital Records Svc Room 217-H 47 Trinity Ave SW Atlanta, GA 30334-5600	(404) 656-4750 Fax: (404) 524-4278 404) 656-4900 Request "long" record	B,D 1919 + Pre-1952 Probate Judge-county M-License issued County Clerk - Superior Ct Earlier records for Atlanta & Savannah- County
I L	IL Div of Vital Records 605 W. Jefferson St. Springfield IL 62702-5097	(217) 782-6553	D, M, Dv - Index Jan 1962+
	Il State Archives Capital Complex M. Cross Norton Bldg Springfield, IL 62756	(217) 782-4682	B-Jan 1916-1943
	E. Illinois Reg Archives Booth Lib E. Illinois Univ Charleston, IL 61920	(217) 581-6093	

K S	Vital Statistics KS Dept of Health 900 SW Jackson St Topeka KS 66612 2221	(913) 296-1400	B, D, M, Dv Jul 1911+ prior County Clerk
M A	Reg of Vital Records 150 Tremont St Rm B-3 Boston, MA 02111	(617) 727-7388	M - 1901+ D - Index 1952+ County Registrar of Probate Ct.
	Mass Archives Columbia Pt 220 Morrissey Blvd. Boston, MA 02125	(617) 727-2816	B , D 1841-1905 M 1841-1905
	Bur of Health Stat 470 Atlantic Av 2nd FL Boston, MA 02210	(617) 753-8600	pre 1841 -town of event Dv: +1952 county
M D	State of Md. Archives 350 Rowe Blvd. Annapolis, MD 21401	(410) 974-3914	B, D + 1898 Baltimore +1875
M D	Div of Vital Records Dept of Health 4201 Patterson Ave PO Box 68760 Baltimore, MD 21215-0020	(301) 225-5988	M-June 1951+ Baltimore- Clerk of Common Pleas Clerk of Court of Common Pleas D-Verification only 1961+ County Clerk of Circuit Ct
		(410) 764-3069 (410) 764-3174	Dv - prior Jan 1961 county

M I	Office of State Registrar Dept. of Comm .Health 3423 N. Logan St. PO Box 30195 Lansing, MI 48909	(517) 335-8666 has internet death index 1867-1874	B& D 1867+ earlier records
	MI Dept of Pub Health	(517) 335-8655	M-April 1867+ D-1897+

	Detroit records
	  Dept of Health-Detroit
	  County Clerk
			B- Detroit 1893+
			D- Detroit 1897+

N
E
	Dept Vital Statistics
	Dept. of Health
	301 Centennial Mall S.
	PO Box 95007
	Lincoln, NE
	    68509-5007
		(402) 471-2871	B, D late 1904 +
			pre 1904 county
			
			M Jan 1909 +
			  pre-1909 county
			D- 1909+
			  District Court

N J	State Dept of Health Bureau of Vital Statistics PO Box CN 370 S. Warren & Market St Trenton, NJ 08625-0370	(609) 292-4087 Fax (609) 392-4292 no genealogical research done	6/ B D & M 1878+ 5/1848-5/1878 pre 1989 +1989 county of event M-June 1878+
	Archives & History Bureau State Library Division State Dept. of Education Trenton, NJ 08625	(609) 292-4087	May 1848- May 1878
N Y	Dept. of Health Vital Records Section Empire State Plaza Tower Bldg. Rm. 244 Albany, NY 12237-0023	(518) 474-3075 (518) 474-3038	1881 B 1880+ D M + 1880-1907 Dv + 1963 County Dv +1847 sealed for 100 yrs.

N Y C	Div. of Vital Records Dept. of Health 125 Worth St PO Box 3776 New York, NY 10007	(212) 619-4530 (212) 693-4637 212 374-8361 212 788-8580 Archives 212 669-8090 Gen'l Help	B 1910+ D 1949+

	NYC Mun. Archives
	31 Chambers St-
	Rm 103
	New York, NY 10007
		212 788-8580	Manhattan: (NY)
			B-Jul 1847/48
			  Jul 1853-1909
			D-1795,
			  1802-04; 1808;
			  1812-1948
			M-Jun 1847-48;
			  Jul 1853-1937
			
			Brooklyn(Kings)
			B- 1866-1909
			D- 1847-53;
			  1857-1948
			M-1866-1937
			
			Bronx:
			B- 1898-1909
			D- 1898-1948
			M- 1898-1937
			Dv- Pre 1949

O H	State Dept of Health 246 N. High St PO Box 15098 Colombus, OH 43215-0098	(614) 466-2531	B- + 12/20/1908 D -+ 12/31/1945 D 1908-1936 county M/Dv-Sept 1949+ State

	Ohio Historical Society Archives Library Div 1985 Velma Avenue Columbus, OH 43211	(619) 297-2510 Online Death Cert 1913-1927	1933-1937 B,D 1909-1945
P A	Vital Records State Dept. of Health Central Building 101 S. Mercer St. P.O.Box 1528 New Castle, PA 16101	(412) 656-3100 Fax (412) 652-8951	B, D Jan 1906+ pre 1906 Register of Wills county B 1870-1905 Pittsburg and Allentown Marriage-county
	Prothonotary Ct Register of Wills City-County Bldg Pittsburg, PA 15219		Dv: county
	Office of Bio-Statistics Health Dept. City-County Bldg. Pittsburgh, PA 15219		1820-1905
	Vital Statistics Dept. of Public Health 401 N. Broad St. Rm. 942 Philadelphia, PA 19108		1860-1915
R I	Dept. of Health 3 Capital Hill Rm. 101 Providence, RI 02908-5097	(401) 222-2811	B, D, M 1853+ 1853-1900 D-1901-1942 Earlier Records Town Clerk Dv 1962+ Dv - 1962

	Historical Society 121 Hope St Providence, RI -2906		
	R.I. State Archives 337 Westminster St Providence, RI 02903		
R I	M- Div of Vital Records RI Dept of Health Rm. 101 Cannon Bldg 3 Capitol Hill Providence, RI 02908-5097 D- Clerk of Family Court 1 Dorrance Plaza Providence RI 02903	(401) 277-2811	Jan 1853+
	Family Court 22 Hayes St Providence, RI 02908		
	Providence College Archives Providence, RI		
V A			M- 1853+ D 1918+M- County Clerk D- County Clerk
T X	Bureau of Vital Statistics PO Box 12040 Austin, TX 78711-2040	(512) 458-7111	B;D 1903+

*J*ewish Genealogical Societies
Special Interest Groups
Jewish Historical Societies

The following abbreviations are used in the tables below
JHS= Jewish Historical Society
JGS= Jewish Genealogical Society
E-Mail= Electronic Mail Address
x + = **www.jewishgen.org+website**

	Society	Address	Telephone- e-mail
A Z	JGS-Arizona Phoenix	Leonard Kamlet. 632 W. Thunderhill Dr Phoenix, Az 85045	(602)460-8229 len@syspac.com
	JHS- S.Arizona	Alfred E. Lipsey 4181 E. Pontatoc Canyon Dr. Tucson, AZ 85718	(520) 299-4486 huhk72a@prodigy.com
C A	JGS-L.A.	Ted Gostin P.O. Box 55443 Sherman Oaks, CA 91343	(818) 786-3239 x+/jgsla
	JGS-Orange Co	Shmuel Fisher 8599 Amazon River Cir Fountain Valley, CA 92708	(714) 968-0395 Shmuel@deltanet.com
	JGS Sacramento	Steve Kitnick 2351 Wyda Way Sacramento CA 95825	(916) 486-0906 x361 x+/jgs-sacramento
	JGS- San Diego	Jackye Sullins P.O. Box 927089 San Diego, CA 92192	(619) 453-8164 jackye@metaflow.com
	JGS/ S.F. Bay Area	Roger Rosenberg P.O. Box 471616 San Francisco, CA 94147	(415) 921-6761 /sfbajgs
C O	JGS- Colorado	Sandra Greenberg P.O. Box 22440 Denver, CO 80222	(303) 755-8384 sangreenb@aol.com

C T	JGS-CT	Jonathan Smith 394 Sport Hill Rd. Easton, CT 06612	(203) 268-2923 70144.3541@ compuserve.com
D C	JGS-Gr. Washington	Roberta Solit P.O. Box 31122 Bethesda, MD 20824	(301) 762-8199 /jgsgw
F L	JGS-Broward	Bernard I. Kouchel P.O. Box 17251 Ft. Lauderdale, FL 33318	(305) 472-5455 koosh@worldnet. att.net
	JGS- Gr. Miami	Ronald Ravikoff PO Box 560432 Miami, FL 33156	jgsmiami@aol.com
	JGS- Gr Orlando	Jay Schleichkorn P.O. Box 941332 Maitland, FL 32794-1332	(407) 862-0043 PTJAY@aol.com
	JGS-Palm Beach Co	Sylvia Nusinov Al B. Leeds P.O. Box 7796 Delray Beach, FL 33482	(561) 483-1060 (561) 496-3354 curiously@aol.com albleeds@aol.com
	JGS- SW Florida	Lorraine Greyson Temple Sinai 1802 Kenilworth St. Sarasota, FL 34238	(914) 924-6468 Lgreys@aol.com
G A	JGS-Georgia	Gary Palgon 2700 Claridge Ct. Atlanta, GA 30360	(770) 458-6664 gmpalgon@aol.com
H I	JGS-Hawaii	Anne Feder Lee 7207 Kuahono St Honolulu HI 96825	(808) 395-0115 AnneLee1@ compuserve.com
I L	JGS- Champaign - Urbana	Dr. Shiela Goldberg 808 La Sell Dr Champagn, IL 61820	(217) 359-3102 sheila@prairienet.or g
	JGS-Illinois Chicago	Larry Hamilton P.O. Box 515 Northbrook, IL 6065	(312) 666-0100 www.jgsi.org

I L /I N	JGS-Illiana	Cleo Courshon PO. Box 384 Flossmoror, IL 60422	(708) 7472805
	JGS- Indianapolis	Jim Borman 1044 Selkirk La Indianapolis IN 46260	(317) 571-8728 jborman@iquest.net
L A	JGS- New Orleans	Jacob Karno 25 Waverly Place Metarie, LA 70003	(504) 888-3817 jkarno@ communique.net
M A	JGS- Gr Boston	Patti Couture Fay Bussgang P.O. Box 610366 Newton Highlands, MA 02161	(617) 796-8522 X+/boston
M D	JHS- Baltimore	Elizabeth S. Carus 3200 Pinkney Rd Baltimore, MD 21215	(410) 732-6400 escarus@ibm.net
M I	JGS -Detroit	Stephen M. Rosman PO Box 251693, W Bloomfield, MI 48325	(248) 355-4212 355-9267 SRosman@aol.com
M O	JGS- St. Louis	Alan Barasch P.O.Box 411571 Louis, MO 63141	(314) 994-1234 www.stlcyberjew. com/jgs-stl
N J	JGS-Central Jersey	Nathan M. Reiss 228 Livingston Av. New Brunswick, NJ 08901	(732) 249-4894 x+/ jhscj
	JGS- North Jersey	Evan Stolbach 1 Bedford Rd Pompton Lakes, NJ 07442	(973201) 839-4045 Estolb7395@ aol.com
	JGS- Morristown	Gary R. Platt 21 Rolling Hill Dr Morristown, NJ 07960	(973) 993-1744 829-0242 pm Fax: 993-1748 grplatt@idt.net

N V	JGS S. Nevada	Schelly Dardashti 205 Surrey St Henderson, NV 89014	(702)896-1899 454-4848 fax 270-2800 dardasht@ ix.netcom.com

	JGS-
	   Las Vegas
		Carole Montello
		P.O.Box 29342
		Las Vegas NV 89626
			(702) 871-9773
			
			scarmont7@
			   juno.com

	JGS- Capital Distric	Norman B. Tillman P.O. box 5002 Albany NY 12205	(518) 462-4815 ntukk10123@aol.co m
	JGS-Buffalo	Dr. Renata Lefcourt 3700 Main St. Amherst NY 14226	(716) 833-0743 lefcourt@local.net
	JGS- Long Island	Jackie Wasserstein 37 Westcliff Dr Dix Hills NY 11746	(516) 549-9532 x+jgsli
	JGS-NYC	Estelle Guzik P.O. Box 6398 New York, NY 10128	(212) 330-8257 http://members.aol.c om/jgsny/main.htm
	JGS- Rochester	Bruce Kahn 265 Viennawood Dr Rochester, NY 14618	(716) 271-2118 x+ /jgsr
O H	JGS- Gr.Cincinnati	Nancy Felson Brant 1580 Summit Rd Cincinnati, OH 45237	(513) 631-0233 nbrant@aol.com
	JGS- Cleveland	Arlene Blank Rich, 996 Eastlawn Drive Highland Heights, OH 44143	(440) 449-2326 fax (216) 621-7650 abr2326@aol.com
	JHS- Columbus	Joseph A. Cohen Peggy H. Kaplan 1175 College Av Columbus, OH 43209	(614) 238-6977 www.gcis.net/cjhs
	JGS Dayton	Dr. Leonard Spialter P.O. Box 338 Dayton OH 45406	(513) 277-3995

O R	JGS-Oregon Portland	David Bernstein MJCC 6651 SW Capitol Hwy Portland, OR 97219	(503) 244-0111 www.teleport.com/~arl/Oregon.html
P A	JGS-Philadelphia	Leonard Markowitz 1279 June Road Huntington Valley, PA 19006	(215) 947-7374 /jgsp
	JGS-Pittsburgh	Julian Falk 2131 Fifth Avenue Pittsburgh, PA 15219	(412) 471-0772 JulFalk@aol.com
T X	Dallas JHS	George Smith 7900 Northaven Road Dallas, TX 75230	(214) 739-2737 X261 dvjcc.ncc.com/dvjccc/DJHS.html
	JGS-Gr. Houston	Dave Fessler 5634 Valkeith Houston, TX 77096	(713) 723-8647 dfessler@prodigy.net
V A	JGS-Tidewater	Kenneth R. Cohen JCC. 7300 Newport Ave Norfolk, VA 23505	(757) 351-2190 kcohen4@juno.com
W I	JGS-Milwaukee	Penny Deshur 9280 N. Fairway Dr Milwaukee, WI 53217	(414) 351-2190 deshur@execpc.com

JGS (Foreign)

COUNTRY	SOCIETY	ADDRESS	E-MAIL / PHONE
Argentina Buenos Aires	AGJA JGS-Argentina	Paul Armony Juana Azurduy 2223 P.8 (1429) Buenos Aires, Argentina 54-1 70-0730	www. geocities.com/Heartland/3402

COUNTRY	SOCIETY	ADDRESS	E-MAIL / PHONE
Australia Sydney	JGS-Australia	AJGS Sophie Caplan P.O. Box 154 Northbridge, Sydney, NSW,1560, Australia	61-3-9578-0368 FAX 61-2- 9967-2834 www.zeta. org.au/ ~feraltek/jozgen. htm
Australia Melbourne	JGS-Melbourne	P.O. Box 189 Glenhuntly, Melbourne Victoria, 3163 Australia	Tel: +61 (03) 9578-0368 www.zeta.org .au/~feraltek/ ajgs.htm
Brazil	SGJB JGS Brasil	Dr. G. Faiguenboim Caisa Postal 1025, 13001-970 Campinas SP, Brazil	(5511) 881-9365 faiguen@ibm. net
Canada Alberta	JGS-S. Alberta	Florence Elman 48 Douglas Park Blvd SE Calgary, Albertra, Canada T2Z 2B1	haflo@ cadvision.com
Montreal	JGS-Montreal	S. M. Diamond 5599 Edgemore Av Montreal, Que, Canada H4w 1V4	(514) 484-0100 fax 484-7306 www.gtrdata. com/jgs~ montreal/
Ottawa	JGS Ottawa	Charles Lapkoff Machzikei Hadas 2310 Virginia Dr Ottawa, ON Canada K1H	(613)723-54-114 lapkoff@ inasec.ca
Toronto	JGS Canada	Henry Wellisch PO Box. 446 Station "A" Willowdale ON Canada M2N 5T1,	(416) 638-3280 Henry_wellisch @tvo.org

COUNTRY	SOCIETY	ADDRESS	E-MAIL / PHONE
Vancouver	JGI-Br. Columbia	Cissie Eppel 950 W.41 Av. #206 Vancouver, BC V5Z 2N7, Canada	(604) 321-9870 www.geocities.com/Heartland/Hills/4441
Winnipeg	JHS W. Canada	JHS-W Canada Bev Rayburn C116 123 Doncaster St Winnipeg, MB R3N 2B2, Canada	(204) 942-4822 www.concentric.net/~lkessler/geninst.shtml
France Paris	GenAmi AGJI	Micheline Gutmann 76 rue de Passy 75016 Paris, France	100766.2212 @compuserve.com
	JGS-France	Cercle de Genealogie Juive Claudie Blamont 14Rue Saint-Lazar, 75009 Paris, France	331-4023-0490 cgigenefr@aol.com
Gr. Britain	JGS-Gr Britain	George Anticoni PO Box 13288 London, N3 3WD, England	44-1923-825-197 Fax: 820-323 www.ort.org/jgsgb
Israel Jerusalem	JGS-Israel	Jean-Pierre Stoweis PO Box 4270 9141 Jerusalem, Israel	972-2-651-4996 fax 671-0269 www.navitek.com/igs
Galil	JGS-Galil	Tali B adar P.O. Box 135 Mizra, 19312 Israel	972-6-642- 9883 talhadar@inter.net.il
Netherlands	NJG	Rudi Cortissos Abbringstraat #1, 1447 PA, Purmerend, Netherlands	0299-644-498 krggenjo@pop.pi.net

COUNTRY	SOCIETY	ADDRESS	E-MAIL / PHONE
S. Africa CapeTown	JGS-Cape Town	Paul Cheifitz PO.Box 541 Sea Point 8060 South Africa	011-442-7048 elion@ iafrica.com
Sweden	JSS-Sweden	Carl H. Carlsson Box 7427, 103 91 Stockholm Sweden	46-8-679-29-17 maynard.gerber @mbox200. swipnet.se
Switzerland		Rene Loeb P.O.B. 2774 CH-8021 Zurich Switzerland	Phone: +41 01-462-78-83 ReneLoeb@ compuserve.com

Special Interest Groups

Country/ Region	Publication webinfo file	Address/ Web site	Telephone/
Galicia	Gesher Galicia ggalicia@ jewishgen.org	Shelley Kellerman Pollero 549 Cypress La Severna Pk, MD 21146	410 647-9492 Fax 315 8188 www1.jewishgen. org/Galicia
Germany	Stammbaum	Karen Franklin Leo Baeck Institute 129 E.73 St. New York, NY 10021	212 744-6400 fax 988-1305 moving 1/99 www.Lbi.org
Grodno Genealogy Group	grodno2@ jewishgen.org	Ellen S Renck Amy Levinson 10 Overlook Rd Scarsdale NY 10583	617 286-8923 http://members. aol.com/ grodsig/ grodsig.htm
Hungary	Magyar Zsido x+/Hungary	Louis Schonfeld PO Box 34152 Cleveland,OH 44134	(216)661-3970
Latvia	Latvia SIG	Marion Werle PO Box 280422 Northridge, CA 91328	x+j/latvia
Lithuania	Litvak SIG members only	Davida Handler PO Box 1387 Cedar Rapids, IA 52403	Fax: 319 363-1071 818 713-8672 x+litvak
Poland	Kielce-Radom	Gene Starn PO Box 520583 Longwood, FL 32752	407 788-3898 x+krsig
	Suwalk, & Lomza Landsmen	Marlene Silverman PO Box 228 3701 Ct Av NW Washington DC 20008	(410) 647-9492 www1. jewishgen.org/ SuwalkLomza

Country/ Region	Publication webinfo file	Address/ Web site	Telephone/
Romania	(Moldova, Bessarabia, Bukovina) ROM-SIG	Gene Starn PO Box 520583 Longwood, FL 32752	407-788-3898 romsig2@ jewishgen.org

The Jewish Genealogical Institute at the Center for Jewish History is slatted for opening early 1999 in New York City. This Institute will combine the resources of the Leo Beck Institute, YIVO, The American Jewish Historical Society, and the Sephardic House. The addresses provided for the Leo Beck And YIVO will be changing. Check the web sites or telephone directories for information for further updates.

Other web sites of interest may be the special interest discussion groups that take place on the internet through Jewishgen. These are generally free.

Go to *Jewishgen.org* then
Regional Special Interest Groups

After a while you will find your own special web sites. These sites are as of August, 1998 and can change.

Notes:

*G*enealogical Hebrew

And other terms

ג ב א

Genealogical Glossary

ahnetafel	pedigree chart in text form
aliyah	return home
ancestry	descendants of one individual
Ashkenazi	persons originating in Germany
bar	aramaic, Hebrew for son of
bat (bas)	Aramaic, Hebrew daughter of
ben	Hebrew for son of
census	recording of information about people by the government; in U.S. required every ten years for apportionment of House of Representatives
data	information
descendant	a person who is descended from someone
diaspora	disperse
direct line	mother, father
download	computer term for exchanging information from one person to another
emigrant	person that leaves one's country to immigrate to another
family chart	a way of recording information about one family
floppy disk	a portable non-permanent disk for recording information on a computer
Galiciana	a Jew from south-western Poland area that was annexed by Austria
gedcom	genealogical exchange of data in a common format.
genealogy	study of ancestry or family lineage

ibn	arabic for son of
immigrant	foreign person arriving in country
Inquisition	Interrogation of Jews in Spain in the attempt to convert them to Christianity
internet	information network that connects academic and government groups from many countries
Ivrim	original name of Hebrews, from people from across the Euphrates river
Kohim	High priest
landslydt	persons from the same town
landsmanshaften	organization of persons from the same town
Levi	attendants to the Kohim
Litvak	a Jew from the Duchy of Lithuania
maternal	descended from the mother's line
microfiche	sheet of film containing several hundred miniaturized documents
microfilm	film on which materials are photographed at a reduced size
naturalization	the process of becoming a citizen
On- line	being on a computer network
once removed	one generation removed from common ancestor
pages of testimony	certification by relatives and friends about the manner of death of Holocaust victims.
Pale of Settlement	Russian restricted geographic area created in 1791 limiting where Jews were allowed to live
paternal	descended from the father's line
pedigree chart	graph for recording of who one is descended from on a direct line

probate	the process of validating a will
progenitor	an ancestor in the direct line
Rashi	Rabbi Shlomo ben Isaac, a great scholar
Rosh Hashana	Celebration of Creation of World
SASE	self addressed stamped envelope
Sephardi	persons originating in Spain, Sephardim (pl)
shadchan	marriage broker
shtetl	a small village or town (Yiddish)
SIG	Special Interest Groups; persons study a specific geographical area
soundex	a numerical code based on the way a name sounds
Ten Lost Tribes	Northern kingdom of Israel tribes
vital record	birth, marriage, death records
world wide web	a network of groups and individuals that exchange information
www	world wide web
yiddish	a dialect of German spoken by East European Jews
Yiskor	remembrance of one's ancestor

The Hebrew Aleph-Bet

א = silent	בּ = B	ג=G	ד=D
ה=H	ו=V	ז=Z	ח=Ch
ט=T	כ=KH	ך= final KH	ל =L
מ =M	ם=final M	נ=N	ן =N
ס=S	ע=silent	כּ=K	פ =P
ף=Final P	צ=Ts	ץ=Final Ts	ק =K
ר =R	ש=Sh	ת =T	י=Y

Hebrew Numerals

1...א	10...י	100...ק
2...ב	20...כ	200...ר
3...ג	30...ל	300...ש
4...ד	40...מ	400...ת
5...ה	50...נ	500...תּ"פ
6...ו	60...ס	600...תּ"
7...ז	70...ע	700...ש"ת
8...ח	80...פ	800...ת"ת
9...ט	90...צ	900... ת"

Selected Hebrew Names

The book *Jewish Personal Names* by Rabbi Shmuel Gorr, is a wonderful source. Rabbi Gorr lists not only the original form of the name, but most of its variants, in both Hebrew and English. Listed below are some of the more common Hebrew names.[1]

Male Names

Abraham	א ב ר ה ם	Joseph	יוסף
Aharon	אהרן	Leib	ליב
Benjamin	בנימין	Lazar	לייזר
Daniel	דאנל	Meir	מאיר
David	דוד	Menachem	מנחם
Eliyahu	עליא	Manashe	מנשה
Emanuel	מנואל	Saul	שאסל
Hayyim	חיים	Samuel	שמואל
Isaac	איציק	Solomon	שלהמה
Israel	אימרל	Tzvi Hirsch	צבי הירש

Female Names

Adel	אבל	Malka	מלכה
Beila	בייל א	Masha	מאשה

---

[1] *Jewish Personal Names;* Rabbi Shmuel Gorr Avotaynu, Inc. 1992

Chaiyyah	ח'ה	Mina	מינא
Chana	חנה	Miriam	מריס
Chavah	חוה	Nahamah	נחמה
Deborah	דברווה	Perel	פערעל
Esther	אסתר	Rachel	רחל
Feige	פייגלע	Rebecca	רבקה
Gittle	גיטעל	Ruth	רות
Hinda	הינדא	Sarah	סרה
Itta	איטע	Sima	שימא
Leah	לאה	Tzviah	צקוה

Holiday	Hebrew Month	Calendar Month
Passover	14-22 Nisan	Late March/April
Lag B'Omer	18 Iyar	May
Shavuot	6 Sivan	May
Tishah be-Av	9 Av.	August
Rosh Hashana	1 Tishri	September
Yom Kippur	10 Tishri	September/October
Sukkoth	15 Tishri	October
Simchat Torah	22 Tishri	October

Holiday	Hebrew Month	Calendar Month
Chanukah	24 Kislev-2 Tevet	December
Purim	14 Adar	March

	Nisan . . . נ י ס ן	Kislev. . ק ס ל ד
Iyar . . א יי ר	Elul. . . . ל ו ל	Tevet.. ת ב ח
Sivan. ס י ד ן	Tishri. . . ת ש רי	Shevat . . שבט
Tammuz. . . . ת מ ו ז	Cheshvan. . . כ ש ב ן	Adar.. א ד ר

APPENDIX

State Census

District of Columbia:

1867, 1878, 1885, 1888, 1894, 1905-1909, 1912-1913, 1915. 1947, 1919, 1925. The 1885-1925 are police censuses.

Florida:

1884:Franklin County only
1868 Leon County Only

Illinois:

1855 Indexed in Illinois Early Records Index
1862 Military index 18-45
1865
1934 Census of Chicago

Kansas:

1855 1859, 1865, 1874, 1875, 1885, 1895. 1905, 1915, 1925 1865--includes military unit 1885 includes military census

Massachusetts:

1855, 1865, 1875, 1885, 1895, 1905, 1912, 1915. 1925, 1935, 1945 1912: Essex County only 1915 Statistics only

Michigan:

1853, 1854, 864, 1866, 1874, 1884, 1894, 1935

Minnesota:

1857, 1865, 1875, 1885, 1895, 1905
1885, 1905 includes Civil War Veterans
1905 includes Spanish American War Veterans

Missouri:

1852, 1856, 1864, 1868, 1876

Nebraska:

1854, 1855, 1856, 1865, 1869. 1885 1885 includes mortality schedules

New Jersey:

1855, 1865, 1875, 1885, 1892, 1905, 1915

New York:
1855, 1865, 1875, 1885, 1892, 1905. 1915. 1925

Ohio:
1851, 1855, 1859, 1863, 1867, 1871, 1875, 1879, 1891, 1895, 1897, 1903, 1907, 1911, 1915

Census Research Worksheet

Soundex Code	Name	Census Year	Index Reel		Census Reel	County	ED	Sheet #	Line #
S-223	Schuster,	1920	M	702	T 625	1183	Kings	14	3	37

Jewish Arrivals in the United States 1649-1900[1]

Alabama

Chaiborne	1840
Mobile	1724
Montgomery	1852*
Selma	1867*
Sheffield	1884

Alaska

Sitka	1868

Arkansas

Fort Smith	1842
Hot Springs	1831
Jonesboro	1882
Little Rock	1838
Pine Bluff	1845

California

Jesu Marie	1850
Los Angeles	1849
Oakland	1866
Sacramento	1853*
San Diego	1860*
San Francisco	1850
San Jose	1875*

Colorado

Denver	1858
Colorado Springs	1890
Pueblo	1899*
Trinidad	1883*

Delaware

New London	1892
Hartford	1843
New Haven	1772
Waterbury	1840
Wilmington	1885

District of Columbia

Washington	1832

Florida

Jacksonville	1882
Miami	1896
Pensacola	1874
Tampa	1894

Georgia

Atlanta	1846
Augusta	1825
Macon	1850
Savannah	1733

Idaho

Boise	1863

Illinois

Aurora	1861
Bloomington	1850
Chicago	1830
Peoria	1847
Pontiac	1856

Indiana

Evansville	1840
Fort Wayne	1830
Kokomo	1845
Indianapolis	1850

Iowa

Dubuque	1833
Des Moines	1873*
Sioux City	1863*

---

[1]

Under Freedom, pamphlet from the Jewish Museum, New York, December 1, 1954
* Approximate date

Kansas

Ber-Sheba	1882
Montefiore	1884
Wichita	1855

Kentucky

Louisville	1814

Louisaiana

New Orleans	1828*
Shreveport	1848

Maine

Bangor	1890 *
Portland	1877*

Maryland

Baltimore	1773

Massachusetts

Boston	1649
Leicester	1777
Springfield	1888
Worcester	1870

Michigan

Grand Rapids	1852
Bad Axe	1883
Detroit	1765
Jackson	1842
Kalamazoo	1846
Lansing	1848

Minnesota

Minneapolis	1866
St. Paul	1849*

Mississippi

Columbus	1836
Natchez	1781

Missouri

Kansas City	1850*
St. Joseph	1850
St. Louis	1821

Montana

Butte	1875
Helena	1864

Nebraska

Omaha	1856

Nevada

Reno	1848*

New Hampshire

New Castle	1693
Portsmouth	1782*

New Jersey

Camden	1702
Elizabeth	1850
Newark	1844
Paterson	1844

New Mexico

Santa Fe	1846

New York

Brooklyn	1683
Buffalo	1835
Elmira	1851
New York	1654
Rochester	1840*
Syracuse	1839
Utica	1830*

North Carolina

Tarboro	1872*

North Dakota

Bismarck	1871
Fargo	1870*
Painted Woods	1882

Ohio

Akron	1850*
Cincinnati	1817
Cleveland	1837
Dayton	1842*

Oklahoma

New Odessa	1882
Portland	1851
Tulsa	1900

Pennsylvania

Aaronburg	1786
Doylestown	1894
Easton	1752
Philadelphia	1745*
Pittsburgh	1830
Reading	1761

Rhode Island

Newport	1658
Providence	1845*

South Carolina

Charleston	1697
Columbia	1786

South Dakota

Cremiux	1882
Sioux Falls	1890

Tennessee

Chattanooga	1850*
Knoxville	1859
Memphis	1845*
Nashville	1845*

Texas

Galveston	1868*
Houston	1854*
Velasco	1831

Utah

Salt Lake City	1880*

Vermont

Burlington	1878

Virginia

Norfolk	1786
Richmond	1779
Alexandria	1878*
Waterview	1882

Washington

Seattle	1887*
Spokane	1890*
Tacoma	1893*

Virgin Islands

St. Thomas	1796*

West Virginia

Wheeling	1848*

Wisconsin

Madison	1850*
Milwaukee	1847*

Wyoming

Cheyenne	1875

Passenger Arrival Worksheet

Passenger's Name	Soundex Code	Index Reel #	Vol. #	Pg.#	Line #	Record Reel #	✓	Ports

Jewish Genetic Diseases

Bloom's Syndrome	Blooms syndrome is an inherited mutant gene affecting one in every 120 Ashkenazi Jews.
Canavan Disease	Majority of patients are of Ashkenazi Jewish descent.
Dubin-Johnson Syndrome	Found in individuals of Jewish **Iranian** descent. The rate is one in every 250.
Familial Mediterranean Fever	Between two to four in 100 Sephardi Jews exhibit symptoms. One in 100 Iraqi/Kurdish will show signs of disease.
Gaucher Disease	One in every 200 Ashkenazi Jews of Eastern and Central Eastern European ancestry are affected by this disease.
Mucolipidosis IV	Most recently recognized Jewish genetic disease.
Nieman-Pick Disease	It is estimated that one in 75 Ashkenazi Jews is affected.
Pentosuria	One in every 200 Jews of Ashkenazi ancestry.
Phenylketonuria	One in 100 Oriental Jews of **Yemeni or Iranian** ancestry.
Riley-Day Syndrome	Affects one in 100 Jews of Ashkenazi descent.
Tay-Sachs Disease	Affects one in every 200 Ashkenazi Jewish newborns.
Thalassemia	Until recently found only in **Oriental** (Yemeni, Iraqi, Kurdish and Iranian) ancestry. The incidence can be as high as one in every 14.
Torsion Dystonia	One in 6,000 persons actually has the disease gene. Thirty percent of the patients had **Balkan** region ancestry while 20 percent were of **Ukrainian** ancestry.

Archaic Medical Terms

Disease	Definition
Agitaus	Tossed about, disturbed mentally.
Apoplexy	Malady, which arrests the powers of sense and motion.
Asphyxia	Suffocation.
Asthenia	Lack of strength, diminution of vital powers, debility.
Bright's Disease	Generic term including several forms of acute and chronic diseases of the kidney.
Cerebral Apoplexy	Referring to the brain.
Cholera	A disorder, attended with diarrhea, vomiting, stomach ache, and cramps.
Cirrhosis	A disease of the liver.
Congestion	The accumulation of blood or morbid matter in any part of the body.
Consumption	Progressive wasting away from pulmonary tuberculosis.
Cytolysis	Disintegration of the cells.
Dementia	Madness, insanity.
Diphtheria	Acute contagious disease of the heart.
Dropsy	Abnormal excess of fluid.
Dysentery	Inflammation of the mucous membrane and glands of the large intestine.
Eclampsia	A sudden convulsive seizure during pregnancy or childbirth.
Edema	See Dropsy.
Endocarditis	Inflammation of the lining of the heart.

Disease	Definition
Enteritis	Inflammation of the intestines.
Ersiphelas	Inflammation of the skin and subcutaneous tissues.
General Debility	Used to describe infants who die soon after birth without any marked disorder or organic defect.
Inanition	Exhausted from want of nourishment.
La Grippe	Influenza.
Marasmus	Wasting away of the body, especially in young children.
Myelitis	Inflammation of the spinal cord.
Nephritis	Inflammation of the kidney.
Neuralgia	An affection of nerves especially of the head and face.
Neurocephalus	Nervous disorder.
Oedema	Variation of edema.
Parechymatus	Inflammation of a gland or organ.
Peritonitis	Inflammation of the abdomen.
Pertussis	Whooping cough.
Phthisic	Pulmonary Tuberculosis.
Puerperal Fever	Infection following childbirth.
Pulmonalia	Disease of the lungs.
Pyaemia	Blood poisoning.
Sarcoma	Malignant tumor
Senile Debility	Old age
Septic Anemia	Septic poisoning.
Spinal Sclerosis	Hardening of spinal tissues.

Disease	Definition
Tetanus	A disease of spasm and rigidity of voluntary muscles caused by a wound or injury.
Tuberculosis	To waste away.
Uremia	Severe kidney disease.

Other archaic medical terms used on older death certificates appears below. [2]

Abscess
Burned
Carbuncle
Cancer
Casualty
Catarrh
Childbed
Chlorosis
Colic
Cramp
Diarrhea
Drinking Cold Water
Frozen
Epilepsy
Fever
Fracture
Hives
Killed or Murdered

Locked Jaw
Measles
Drowned
Mortification
Palsy
Pleurisy
Riickets
Rheumatism
Passion
Small Pox
Sore Throat
Stillborn
Stones
Suicide
Scurvy
Teething
Worms

[2]New York City Archives

Family Health History

Disease	Father	Mother	Sibling	Sibling	GF (M)	GM (M)	GF (P)	GM (P)
Asthma								
Cancer(Type)								
Breast Cancer								
Alzheimer Disease								
Parkinson								
Diabetes								
Glaucoma/Macular Degeneration								
Heart Disease/Stroke								
Birth Defect								
High Blood Pressure								
Tuberculosis								
Osteoporosis								
Other:								

City Directories Chart

Name:_____

Year	City	Street Address	Occupation
1880		h. w.	
1890/92		h. w.	
1895		h. w.	
1900		h. w.	
1905		h. w.	
1910		h. w.	
1915		h. w.	
1920		h. w.	
1925		h. w.	
1930		h. w.	
Current		h.	

h=home address
w=work address

-N-

Address Directory/Correspondence Log

Name	Address	City, State, Zip	Telephone #	

Family Questionnaire

You

Your Birth NAME _____

Your Hebrew NAME _____

For Whom were you named _____

Your Birth Date _____

Birth Address _____

Borough/City _____

County _____

Spouse

Birth name of SPOUSE _____

(in marriage that produced children)

Hebrew NAME _____

For Whom were you named _____

Date of Birth _____

Date of Marriage: _____ City _____

County _____

Other Marriages:

Birth Name of SPOUSE _____

Date of Marriage _____ City _____

County _____

Name of Landsmanshaften or Fraternal Organizations:

Name of Synagogue:

Paternal:

1895 Address _____

1900 Address _____

1905 Address _____

1900 Address _____

1910 Address _____

1915 Address _____

1920 Address _____

1925 Address _____

1930 Address _____

Maternal:

1895 Address _____

1900 Address _____

1905 Address _____

1900 Address _____

1910 Address _____

1915 Address _____

1920 Address _____

1925 Address _____

1930 Address _____

Notes:

Soundex Coding Guide

1 = B P F V
2 = C S K G J Q X Z
3 = D, T
4 = L
5 = M, N
6 = R

Soundex Code	Surname
S-632	Schwartz